The Solution of the Fist

The Solution of the Fist

Dostoevsky and the Roots of Modern Terrorism

John P. Moran

LEXINGTON BOOKS

A division of
ROWMAN & LITTLEFIELD PUBLISHERS, INC.
Lanham • Boulder • New York • Toronto • Plymouth, UK

LEXINGTON BOOKS

A division of Rowman & Littlefield Publishers, Inc.
A wholly owned subsidiary of The Rowman & Littlefield Publishing Group, Inc.
4501 Forbes Boulevard, Suite 200
Lanham, MD 20706

Estover Road
Plymouth PL6 7PY
United Kingdom

British Library Cataloguing in Publication Information Available

Library of Congress Cataloging-in-Publication Data

Moran, John P.
The solution of the fist : Dostoevsky and the roots of modern terrorism / John P. Moran.
p. cm.
Includes bibliographical references and index.
ISBN 978-0-7391-2985-2 (cloth : alk. paper) -- ISBN 978-0-7391-2986-9 (pbk.)
1. Terrorism--Psychological aspects. 2. Dostoyevsky, Fyodor, 1821-1881. I. Title.
RC569.5.T47M67 2009
363.325'3--dc22 2009007249

Printed in the United States of America

™ The paper used in this publication meets the minimum requirements of American National Standard for Information Sciences—Permanence of Paper for Printed Library Materials, ANSI/NISO Z39.48–1992.

To

Maria Clarita Ferrer Moran
Patrick Ferrer Moran
Megan Versoza Moran

My life would be empty and meaningless without you.

Contents

Acknowledgements

The complementary nature of writing and thinking is difficult to understand and describe. It is just as difficult to disaggregate the many outside influences that bear upon this process. Any effort to isolate a single influence often results in the neglect of another. Such is the unfortunate tendency of the human mind.

With this in mind, I will attempt to thank those individuals who have been enormously helpful to me in this challenging but highly rewarding project.

I must thank, first and foremost, Dr. Mark Kremer. His singularly insightful interpretation of Rousseau's long-forgotten but crucially important novel, *La Nouvelle Heloise*, radically transformed my ideas about Dostoevsky. He has graciously and selflessly spent hours of his time in discussion with me about this. I am fortunate and honored to be his colleague. He is unquestionably the most gifted political theorist of our generation.

I would also like to thank the two individuals who, perhaps unbeknownst to them, first gave me the idea for this project. The first is my triplet brother and long-time Federal and State prosecutor, William Taylor, Esq., who once said to me, "If you truly want to understand the criminal mind, you must read Dostoevsky." The second is a friend, shipmate, and Middle East expert, Dr. David Wurmser, who further enticed me down the Dostoevskian road one day by telling me, "If you want to understand today's terrorists, you must read Dostoevsky."

I believe that Dostoevsky understands the criminal and terrorist minds because he understands the human soul, an aspect of human reality largely ignored in our modern, scientific era. With this in mind, I must thank several individuals who helped me to appreciate the forces of the human soul: Dr. Carl Linden, my mentor who, through intellect and heart, guided me through the scientific shoals of political science; Dr. Larisa Naumovna Neustadt and Aleksander Neustadt, who first introduced me to the warmth and generosity of the Russian soul; and Carlos and Petronila Ferrer ("Nanay" and "Tatay"), the grandparents of my children, who show an unrivaled commitment to their family and loved ones. All of these people exhibit a selflessness of soul that would impress Dostoevsky himself.

I would also like to thank the following people who had an indirect, but important, influence upon the evolution of my ideas: U.S. Representative Christopher P. Carney (D-PA), Stephen McKelvey (Kennesaw State University), Amy Devlin, Terrence Casey (Rose-Hulman Institute of Technology), Khalil Habib (Salve Regina University), Peter Lawler (Berry College), Katya Vladimirov (Kennesaw State University), Meyrav Wurmser (Hudson Institute), Matthew Hoffman (University of Toronto), Joe Head (Kennesaw State University), Fr. Deogracias Rosales, Michael Ricke, and Dr. Virginia Taylor (d'Aragon).

I have been blessed in my life through an association with hundreds of other wonderful people. I regret that I can not mention them all. However, the last person I must thank is the person I should have thanked first, my mother, Mary Alice McManus. She is a life-long educator who not only selflessly raised me but deftly instilled in me an appreciation of learning and thinking. This is no easy feat in our harried and unreflective world.

Chapter 1
Terrorism in the Age of Reason

There are moments in history in which the true nature of a thing is easy to discern. This usually occurs at the beginning of such a thing. It is for this reason that Fyodor Mikhailovich Dostoevsky was blessed with timing, for not only did he witness the rapid economic modernization of Russia during the late nineteenth century, but also the blossoming of modern terrorism.

Although terrorism was born in Europe, Imperial Russia was its cradle. In the early 1860's there were no more than one hundred terrorists in Russia. By 1907, the number of terrorists in Russia had increased to an astounding 45,000.[1] The number of successful attacks also increased proportionately: from two failed attacks in the 1860's, to about thirty-five successful assassinations between 1877-1881. By the 1904-1907 timeframe, the number of assassinations increased to 209.[2] In the period between 1905-1908, 2,563 government personnel were killed by terrorists and an additional 2,954 were wounded.[3]

Dostoevsky had the advantage of witnessing terrorism in its infancy. Terrorists of his day had yet to develop the convoluted morality of today's terrorists. They were, in fact, self-proclaimed nihilists. Sergei Nechaev made this rather clear in 1869 in his *Catechism of the Revolutionist*, a document that remains a foundational work for modern terrorism. In it he writes,

> In the very depths of his being, not only in words but also in deeds, he [the revolutionary terrorist] has broken every tie with the civil order and the entire cultured world, with all its laws, proprieties, social conventions, and its ethical rules. He is an implacable enemy of this world, and if he continues to live in it, that is only to destroy it more effectively.[4]

Terrorists today rarely admit to being nihilists. In fact, they rarely admit to being terrorists at all, preferring labels such as "freedom fighter" or "guerilla."[5] This, in itself, is testament to the moral discomfort felt by terrorists. Rather than to admit that innocent people are killed in the name of a political cause, terrorists cloak their activities in the language of a "just war" and assume that all human beings are potential combatants within it.

Strikingly, this is an evolution of thought that is widely accepted today both within terrorist circles as well as with the general public. In this regard, terrorism has become something akin to a middle-aged man who has convinced himself and others that he is something he is not. Gone is the clarity of his infancy during which his fundamentally violent and nihilistic essence was clear to all.

Today we have not only lost Dostoevsky's unsullied perspective on terrorism, but his *paradigm*. As products of the age of reason, we attempt to understand terrorism in scientific manner. We attempt to separate fact from value in an effort to isolate the observable and measurable causal variables of terrorism. Unfortunately, this is an endeavor that has been strikingly ineffective in understanding anything but the most obvious aspects of modern terrorism.[6]

Dostoevsky was not a social scientist. In fact, as will be seen below, he was not only extremely suspicious of the dehumanizing influences of science upon society, but skeptical about its ability to accurately understand it. It is for this reason that he approached terrorism in a distinctly non-scientific manner—a manner which enables us to get to the root of the two riddles confounding those who attempt to understand terrorism scientifically.

The Riddles Confounding Us

Two riddles continue to puzzle those attempting to understand terrorism in a scientific manner—one *political*, and one *psychological*. The political riddle touches upon the fact that terrorism is a strikingly new phenomenon. Simply speaking, terrorism is a *modern* phenomenon. Three pre-modern terrorist groups are often presented to counter this claim—the Thugs, the Assassins, and the Zealots. All three groups, however, were clearly motivated by *divine* rather than *political* causes.[7] This is in direct contrast to today's terrorists who commit violent acts in the name of a *political* cause. Even though there are significant differences with regard to the way in which "terrorism" is defined, a consensus has emerged that terrorism is violence (or threatened violence) in the pursuit of *political* change.[8]

As history illustrates that violence is not the creation of the nineteenth century, we must logically examine the other variable in the terrorist equation—the political ideas over which the terrorists became violent in this period. What are these ideas? How are they responsible for the birth of this new politically violent method? As we shall see, this is a riddle that Dostoevsky addresses directly.

The second riddle confounding the scientific analysts of terrorism, a *psychological* riddle, deals with the human conscience and the difficulties that virtually all human beings have in killing other human beings. Few can deny that getting human beings to kill other human beings is an exceedingly difficult task. Those in the business of killing—most notably militaries—have spent years trying to figure out how to overcome this taboo. Recently, Dave Grossman analyzed a study that was done during World War II in which combat-hardened soldiers were asked about their combat experience. It was discovered, based upon interviews with thousands of soldiers who had fought in both the Pacific and European theaters that on average only 15 to 20 percent actually used their weapons while in combat.[9] These combat veterans did not refuse to fire out of cowardice, ". . . but they simply would not fire their weapons at the enemy, even when faced with repeated waves of banzai charges."[10] Grossman concluded that there is, ". . . within most men an intense resistance to killing their fellow man. A resistance so strong that, in many circumstances, soldiers on the battlefield will die before they can overcome it."[11] The mere fact that militaries devote so much time, effort, and money to training soldiers how to kill in battle indicates that there very well may be a natural aversion to killing which is hardwired into human beings.

This being the case, it is surprising that more research has not been done in order to understand how terrorists overcome this natural resistance to killing other human beings. Indeed, terrorists are not simply killing others under hostile fire, but are engaged in the killing of innocent civilians in such mundane places as shopping malls and cafes. They are able to do this without the ample resources that many national militaries have—yet they remain surprisingly successful at it.

A strict adherence to the scientific principles of *objectivity*, *verifiability*, and *quantification* within social science has handicapped us in addressing these two riddles.[12] This is due to the nature of the riddles themselves. They occupy the world of ideas and human conscience. Quantification of these is particularly difficult. How does one measure or quantify a political idea such as freedom or equality? How can it help us to understand the tradeoffs that are often required in balancing these two ideals? Even more challenging for the scientific investigator is an examination of the concept of human guilt—an emotion which derives from a belief system of good and bad. Science does not take into account values or belief systems. It never claims to. This makes it a particularly poor tool with which to understand them.[13]

Dostoevsky's great advantage here is that he pre-dates the scientific revolution within the social sciences. In fact, he felt that science was not merely an incomplete method with which to understand the political world around us, but an actual threat to it. In taking the *values* out of the human decision making process, science creates a world of destructive nihilists. For Dostoevsky, science was not merely a method by which some attempt to understand the world, but had itself become a player in shaping the world around it.

The Political Roots of Terrorism

Dostoevsky first and foremost understood terrorism to be a political act.[14] In this regard, he is not viewed by today's scholars as being particularly revolutionary in thought. Indeed, as already mentioned, terrorism is commonly seen today as a violent method by which individuals pursue political change.[15]

Dostoevsky distinguishes himself from today's thinkers, however, by focusing upon the political *roots* of terrorism. In his day, there were two political causes embraced by terrorists: ethno-nationalism and revolutionary socialism. Revolutionary terrorists primarily based their "cause" upon socialist or left-wing principles, promising to pursue egalitarian *economic* principles once political power was achieved through their violent means. Ethno-national terrorists, on the other hand, advocated the establishment of a state based upon ethnic or cultural boundaries, the goal of which was the creation of a *culturally* homogenous state.[16] To state it another way, they demanded adherence to that dangerously just-sounding maxim that, "every nation has the right to self-determination."

The terrorists' attraction to these two seemingly opposed ideologies waxed and waned throughout the nineteenth and twentieth centuries. After the initial burst of ethno-national terrorist activity in Central Europe in the 1840's, revolutionary socialism gained in its appeal, climaxing ultimately in Tsarist Russia. After a brief hiatus, ethno-national terrorist activity revived in the anti-colonial movement following the Second World War. Revolutionary terrorism returned in the 1960's with groups like the Red Army Faction and the Red Brigades, and ceased only after the collapse of communism in Central Europe and the Soviet Union in 1989 and 1991 respectively.

In the late twentieth century, we see the emergence of an ideological offshoot of ethno-nationalism that is sometimes known as "religious terrorism." Terrorist groups like Hamas, Hezbollah, and al Qaeda are "religious" insofar as the language of their discourse. Their terrorist activities, however, are not directed at affecting *religious* change, but *political* change. Leaders of these groups see themselves as the political leaders of a nation defined in religious terms. They are, essentially, religious nationalists.

The last twentieth century ideology that attracted the attention of the terrorist method was environmentalism.[17] These "ecoterrorists" are diverse in their specific orientation, however they share the common goal of protecting "nature" through violent means. They may be fighting to stop laboratory testing of animals, the hunting of animals in the wild, the preservation of a clean environment, or a natural (non-technological) lifestyle. In many cases, they are willing to harm or sacrifice human life in order to save animal life.

What is often overlooked is that the underlying spirit of these four causes is grounded in the political ideal of *equality*. This is obvious with regard to left-wing causes, but not immediately obvious with regard to ethno-national causes. As Benedict Anderson makes so clear, the first roots of ethno-nationalism are found in the Creole communities of the colonial Americas. He writes, "Even if he [the Creole] was born within one week of his father's migration, the accident of birth in the Americas consigned him to subordination—even though in terms of language, religion, ancestry, or manners he was largely indistinguishable from the Spain-born Spaniard."[18] The Creole demand for political equality morphed into the creation of a new "Peruvian," "Brazilian," or "American" identity separate from that of the mother country. This Creole imperative, augmented by the cultural conditions found in Europe, created the conditions for the rise in European ethno-nationalism. From this point onward, equality would not be predicated upon birth. All cultures—great and small—would be equals in the great panoply of the world's diverse cultures.

Because politicized religious movements, like Islamism, are nothing more than religious nationalism, it is equally as clear that the principle of equality provides the core element for this movement as well. The political zeal of the Islamist is not based solely upon a religious zeal. Such a person could easily confine himself to a quiet life of religious contemplation. His zeal is powered by a demand for "justice"—a justice predicated upon its modern prerequisite—equality.

The 1998 fatwa of Osama bin Laden, leader of al Qaeda, is a classic statement in this regard. In this statement, bin Laden justifies his declaration of war against "Jews and Crusaders" by focusing upon the unjust treatment of Muslims worldwide. His grievances were three-fold: 1) An objection to the "occupation" by the United States of the holiest of places of Islam within the Arabian Peninsula, 2) An objection to then UN-sponsored sanctions on Iraq, and 3) An objection to U.S. support for Israel, a non-Muslim state which occupies Jerusalem and "murders" Muslims. These three grievances are distinctly political (as opposed to religious) and highlight the oppression by non-Muslims of Muslims.[19] Bin Laden never focuses upon unjust Muslim-run regimes except to complain that such (unjust) Muslim leaders are actually agents of non-Muslim countries and apostates.[20]

Ecoterrorists have similarly embraced the spirit of justice through equality. In this regard, they see no difference in the application of the principal of equality whether it is to man or to nature. Just as many current medical testing procedures would preclude most human-subject testing, so the animal rights groups would preclude such testing upon animals. One such organization, the Animal Liberation Front, writes on its website,

> The men and women of the Animal Liberation movement pattern themselves after the freedom fighters in Nazi Germany who liberated war prisoners and Holocaust victims and destroyed equipment—such as weapons, railways, and gas ovens that the Nazis used to torture and kill their victims. Other comparisons would include the anti-Apartheid movement, led by Nelson Mandela, who used and supported violence in the fight for liberation in South Africa, and the current struggle by Palestinians against their Israeli oppressors.[21]

The fact that all of these terrorist causes have a common root in equality explains yet another riddle of modern terrorism: why is it that terrorists leap so easily from one ideological cause to another? The most famous case study in this regard is Ilich Ramirez Sanchez, otherwise known as "Carlos the Jackal." At various times in his career he embraced rather different ideologies. He was initially motivated by leftist ideology, purportedly sponsored by Fidel Castro. He later embraced ethno-nationalism, specifically supporting the Popular Front for the Liberation of Palestine (PLFP). After his capture and imprisonment in France, he has embraced the Islamist cause of Osama bin Laden.

Such a terrorist career should be ideologically impossible if terrorist causes did not have a common root. Ramirez Sanchez is not unique; others have vacillated between seemingly contradictory causes in order to continue with their terrorist careers. Even such long-standing terrorist groups such as the IRA (Irish Republican Army) and ETA (the Basque separatist group *Euskadi ta Askatasuna*) have embraced either nationalist or socialist ideologies at different times in their histories.[22]

Importantly, the adherence to the principle of equality by these terrorist groups does not immediately imply that they are "democratic" in nature or that they are acting primarily in the "name of the people." To state it differently, none of these causes are democratic in the sense that they are fundamentally committed to the *twin* principles of political freedom and legal equality. In fact, each of these broad movements adheres to a form of equality which actually interferes with the notion of political freedom. The left-wing radical's pursuit of *material* equality precludes an individual's freedom to pursue wealth as well as the freedom to own private property. The imperative of the ethno-national terrorist and religious extremist groups for *cultural* equality not only precludes the freedom of those minorities that do not adhere to the official cultural requirements, but restricts the cultural practices of the majority to an "officially approved" version of "the people's" cultures. The environmentalists' demands for *existential* equality (of all living being) infringes upon a whole series of freedoms commonly associated with economic development and human health. Such distorted forms of equality (at least from a liberal perspective) can only occur with the destruction of political freedoms that are seen as basic by modern liberal democracies.

What the concept of freedom was to the eighteenth century, so was the concept of equality to the nineteenth century.[23] Dostoevsky was acutely aware of the newness of this egalitarian revolution and deeply concerned that it would be corrupted by self-interested revolutionaries. Like many other observers of the time, he felt that an equality which neglects freedom ends in despotism. As we shall see, in his novel, *The Demons*, he makes it quite clear that the "common cause," frequently referred to by the novel's terrorists but never defined, is nothing but a fiction.[24] Indeed, when Pyotr Stepanovich Verkhovensky, the terrorist cell leader, is pressured to explain his "cause," he admits that he is not really a socialist, but a "swindler." (10:324)[25] He only claims to be acting in the name of the people; in actuality, he is only interested in personal power.

Today we have lost this perspective. Popular culture tends to view many terrorists as "freedom fighters." Young bohemians sport the image of Che Guevara on their T-shirts and Hollywood glamorizes the life of Ilich Ramirez Sanchez ("Carlos the Jackal") seemingly oblivious to the despotic purposes of their terrorist causes. A close re-read of Dostoevsky's writings might disabuse popular culture of the falsity of such romantic terrorist mirages.

The Psychological Roots of Terrorism

Dostoevsky's understanding of the human psyche was so insightful so as to compel Friedrich Nietzsche to write that, "Dostoevsky was the only psychologist from whom I had anything to learn."[26] Sigmund Freud himself is reputed to have once said that everything he had discovered in the first seventy years of his life had already been found in the works of Fyodor Dostoevsky.[27] In spite of these endorsements, few today turn to Dostoevsky in an effort to understand the psychological motivations of terrorists. This is unfortunate, for he seems to have understood something about the *motivations* of terrorists that few today consider.[28]

Today, the most popular explanation for the motivations of terrorists is known as the "Rational Actor Approach." Scholars who embrace this approach argue that study after study has indicated that, "terrorist activity is not due to mental pathologies."[29] Terrorists have simply come to the conclusion that terrorism as a political method works. One prominent scholar writes, "What limited data we have on individual terrorists . . . suggest that the outstanding common characteristic of terrorists is their normality."[30] In essence, terrorists are disturbingly "normal" in their rational calculations. They simply engage in a process of cost-benefit analysis, and conclude that they can get what they demand by engaging in terrorism. Even suicide terrorists are seen as rational actors in this light.[31]

A similar explanation can be found in a model known as the "Developmental Model," which argues that terrorists simply develop into terrorists as a part of an increasingly violent crescendo of criminal activities.[32] One scholar writes, "Terrorism, in this view, is not the product of a single decision but the end result of a dialectical process that gradually pushes an individual toward a commitment to violence over time."[33] Ehud Sprinzak writes that, "None of the known terrorist groups started its career by the application of terrorism. Most modern terrorists had reached their terrorism *gradually. They had been radicalized into it.*"[34]

Yet another popular explanation for terrorist motivation is known as the "Frustration-Aggression Model," which assumes that human beings commit violent acts out of passion. It focuses upon the frustration and consequent aggression seen by individuals who experience a gap between rising expectations and the lack of satisfaction individuals experience when these expectations are not met. Because their expectations are not met, they lash out violently.[35]

These three explanations are logical, but they do not adequately explain the extreme nature of terrorism. As mentioned above, militaries devote untold millions in order to psychologically train their soldiers to kill the enemy on the battlefield. Few terrorist organizations have such resources, yet they kill with seeming ease. How are they able to psychologically overcome the obstacle of human conscience?

The one current model which adequately addresses this riddle is known as the "Narcissistic Personality Disorder Model." While admitting that most terrorists are not psychopaths, scholars who adhere to this model argue that, ". . . political terrorists are driven to commit acts of violence as a consequence of psychological forces, and that their special psycho-logic is constructed to rationalize acts they are psychologically compelled to commit."[36] According to this model, terrorists are particularly reliant upon the psychological mechanisms of "externalization" and "splitting." Individuals whose childhood development is shaped by a particular type of psychological damage acquire narcissistic wounds.[37] These wounds compel the individual to split out those elements of their psychological makeup that they dislike, externalize them, and then lash out at those individuals who represent an external embodiment of them.

Data supporting the narcissistic personality disorder model with regard to terrorist motivations is difficult to find. The most convincing empirical data illustrates that terrorists are disproportionately from backgrounds of familial disruption. One such study points out that 79 percent of leftist terrorists from the Red Army faction reported severe childhood conflict. Of these, 33 percent reported conflicts with parents.[38] He adds that these terrorists tended to describe the father, when present, ". . . in hostile terms."[39]

Because the collection of data on terrorists is so difficult, it can be enormously useful to examine a group of individuals who are quite similar to terrorists in terms of their proclivity to violence—imprisoned violent criminals. In one important way, murderers and terrorists are similar—they have both killed. Terrorists have done so in the name of a political idea, criminals for a variety of other reasons. However, they both must deal with the psychological cost of killing another human being.

In a recent article, James Gilligan makes an argument very similar to the narcissistic personality disorder model, which focuses upon imprisoned violent criminals. In essence, Gilligan argues that shame can play an important role in motivating individuals to commit violence against other human beings.[40] By observing violent criminals in prison, Gilligan writes that violence, ". . . appears to be committed by people who are so tormented by feelings of being shamed and disrespected by their enemies that they are willing to sacrifice their bodies and their physical existence to replace those intolerable feelings with the opposite feelings of pride and self-respect, and of being honored and admired by their allies and at least respected by their enemies."[41]

Gilligan argues that shame is, at its very core, the lack of self-love. He writes, "Why is child abuse humiliating and shame-inducing to the child? Because it is the clearest possible way of communicating to the child that the parent does not love him (or her). Just as pride means self-love . . . shame means the lack or deficiency of self-love."[42] Gilligan continues by arguing that there are two possible sources of self-love—internal and external. He writes, "While the self-esteem of adults who have attained internalized sources of pride can survive the withdrawal of love from others, up to a point, it appears to be difficult if not impossible for a child to gain the capacity for self-love without first having been loved by at least one parent, or parent-substitute. And when the self is not loved, by itself or by another, it dies, just as surely as the body dies without oxygen."[43]

This intense form of shame, resulting in the "death of the self," can then result in violence. It is, if you will, death of self through the death of self-love. Gilligan found that the most violent men that he worked with had experienced humiliation repeatedly in childhood. They were, "taunted, teased, ridiculed, rejected, insulted."[44] The subsequent shame is converted to rage, which ends in violence. He writes, ". . . people resort to violence when they feel that they can wipe out shame only by shaming those who they feel shamed them."[45] Violence against an individual is the most intense form of shaming someone.

Gilligan also alludes to the fact that individuals may very well commit acts of violence even against those who had nothing to do with their humiliation. They do this to test their "self-dead" status. He writes, "What many of these men have told me is that they themselves had died—meaning that their personalities had died—long before they began killing other people. What they mean by that is that they felt dead inside: empty, numb, without the capacity to feel anything, neither emotions (such as love, fear, or remorse) not even physical sensations."[46] He continues that, "Many described committing the most horrific atrocities in order to see if they could feel anything, and were surprised and disappointed to see that even that did not restore a capacity to have feelings and feel alive."[47]

Is it possible that terrorists who commit atrocities have been so humiliated that they lash out violently? Is it possible that they are psychologically self-dead? Does their self-dead status enable them to continue to kill innocent civilians as a means to test whether they are still alive? If this is the case, why have we seen this truly emerge only in the nineteenth century?

Walter Laqueur, one of the West's leading terrorism experts argues that Dostoevsky's *The Demons* can help us to answer questions such as these. He writes, "In any attempt to understand the psychology and the motives of people with such a predisposition [toward terrorism], the literature of the last century is of more help than the textbooks of forensic medicine."[48] Unfortunately, his discussion of *The Demons* lasts only a few lines. The remaining five chapters of this book are devoted to addressing this in greater depth.[49]

Dostoevsky in Historical Context

Not only did nineteenth century Russia provide a fertile venue to observe the blossoming of modern terrorism, but Dostoevsky's personal tragedies enabled him to experience and observe the most extreme of political and psychological behaviors. Born in 1821 in Moscow, Dostoevsky's mother died when he was sixteen, his father when he was eighteen (presumably murdered by his own peasants). In his youth he was politically radical and became involved in the now-famous Petrashevsky circle. In 1849 he was sentenced to death for involvement in this subversive group. His sentence was famously commuted at the last moment through Tsarist reprieve, and he was sentenced to penal servitude in

Siberia. While there, he had a conservative and religious transformation. He emerged from Siberia an Orthodox believer and Tsarist supporter.

In 1859 he returned to St. Petersburg and, over the next seven years, he experienced a measure of professional success amidst continuing personal tragedy. The most significant among these tragedies occurred in 1864, with the deaths of his wife and brother. This same year he descended into a degree of debt from which he would never escape.

In spite of these setbacks, or perhaps because of them, it was during this period, a period called by Joseph Frank the "miraculous years," that Dostoevsky wrote his greatest works.[50] In 1866 he published *Crime and Punishment*, in 1867, *The Gambler*. Dostoevsky's three other major novels emerged in quick succession: *The Idiot* (1868), *The Demons* (1871), and *The Brothers Karamazov* (1879-1880). He died in 1881.

We are often reminded that Dostoevsky was inspired to write *The Demons* based upon the true story of the murder of a young Russian revolutionary named Ivanov, who was suspected by his fellow conspirators of disloyalty to the revolutionary cause. The leader of this conspiratorial group was the aforementioned Sergei Nechaev, perhaps the most famous of all Russian revolutionary terrorists of this period. Having killed Ivanov, Nechaev had his body dumped into a pond and fled to Switzerland. Upon his return to Russia, he was arrested, tried, and convicted of Ivanov's murder. He died in the Petropavlovsk Fortress in 1883.

The plot of *The Demons* roughly parallels this series of events—at least up to a point. The action takes place in 1870 in a fictitious, provincial Russian town (named Skvoreshniki). Four characters dominate the action within this novel, two from the "younger" generation, and two from the "older" generation. The two younger characters are Pyotr Stepanovich Verkhovensky (the character based upon Sergei Nechaev) and Nikolai Vsevolodovich Stavrogin (the character based upon Petrashevsky colleague Nikolai Speshnev).[51] The two older characters are Pyotr Stepanovich's widowed father Stepan Trofimovich Verkhovensky (a character based upon a Russian historian of the 1840's, T. N. Granovsky) and Nikolai's widowed mother Varvara Petrovna Stavrogina.[52]

The novel begins with an excruciatingly long description of the dysfunctional relationship of Stepan Trofimovich and Varvara Petrovna. Taking up almost the first fifth of the novel, Dostoevsky expertly paints a picture of two neurotic, self-absorbed, indulgent, nineteenth century Russian "liberal" intellectuals living in a small town in the Russian countryside. Stepan Trofimovich is the hired tutor for her son, Nikolai Vsevolodovich. Throughout the novel, the relationship between Stepan Trofimovich and Varvara Petrovna seems to precariously teeter between friendship and romance, although it never becomes physically amorous. As the years progress, Stepan Trofimovich becomes completely reliant upon Varvara Petrovna for everything that an actual mother would provide (food, shelter, and emotional support). This maternal role appears to be one that Varvara Petrovna, at least superficially, seems happy to play. Stepan Trofimovich, on the other hand, is not only in need of this, but seems quite content to be her child. The irony here is that both have actual children of their own, yet seem utterly negligent in functioning as genuine parents to either of them.

The action of the novel begins as the two sons, Pyotr Stepanovich and Nikolai Vsevolodovich return home from abroad. Each son upsets the order of things in a different way. Nikolai Vsevolodovich, a strikingly handsome and unpredictable young man, creates a series of scandals either through womanizing or through unpredictable behavior. The first factor is particularly noteworthy insofar as we learn, as the novel unfolds, that Nikolai is secretly married to Marya Timofeevna Lebyadkina (the lame, mentally ill sister of the town drunk), while having had or having affairs with three other women in town—Marya Ignateevna Shatova (the wife of the victim of the future plot conspiracy), Darya Pavlovna Shatova (the sister of the victim of the future plot conspiracy), and Lizaveta Nikolaevna Tushina (the bright young woman favored by the novel's narrator). While Nikolai Vsevolodovich causes enormous pain and suffering to virtually all of the female characters, he is not a terrorist as such.[53]

Peter Stepanovich, on the other hand, is a terrorist. He is the head of a small terrorist cell, a "group of five," which is committed to a revolutionary "common cause." Importantly, it is never made completely clear what the end goal of this revolution would be. In fact, the revolutionaries themselves are a motley collection of individuals with quite different ideological orientations. Among the group we find such diverse ideological backgrounds as a Fourierist, a Slavophile, a progressive idealist, and a liberal Westernizer.

In terms of group cohesion, this diversity of ideological backgrounds represents a managerial challenge to the group leader—Pyotr Stepanovich. Halfway through the novel, Nikolai Vsevolodovich suggests to Pyotr Stepanovich that the best means to cement this diverse group together is to commit a murder in which every member of the "group of five" would be implicated. This idea appeals to Pyotr Stepanovich.[54] He has a victim ready—Ivan Pavlovich Shatov (the Slavophile)—a character who has already expressed his desire to leave the terrorist cell.

From this point onward, the "common cause" is put on the back burner and the main conspiracy to which Pyotr Stepanovich and the others commit their energies is to the murder of Shatov. Ultimately, Shatov is murdered. Unfortunately for Pyotr Stepanovich, this does not have the desired "cementing" effect on the group. It does quite the opposite. The cell members are so traumatized by the murder that through confession, hysteria, and implication, they are arrested. Only Pyotr Stepanovich escapes arrest by leaving town immediately.

Toward the end of the novel, Stepan Trofimovich reappears. The events surrounding this conspiracy seem to have caused him to have an emotional breakdown (among other things). In this unstable condition, he leaves Skvoreshniki on his "final" quest, alone, and on foot. He soon thereafter meets up with a holy woman who aids and comforts him. Varvara Petrovna, having learned of his departure, chases him down, and eventually finds him. The two are reunited and declare their mutual love. Stepan Trofimovich then dies. Having lost this proxy son/would-be lover, Varvara returns home only to discover that her real son, Nikolai Vsevolodovich, who was rumored to have traveled to St. Petersburg after the murders, is in fact hanging dead from the rafters of her home. In the last line of the novel, Dostoevsky hints that this suicide was not the result of "insanity."

The Demons is a difficult book to read for the modern reader. Some readers find themselves lost amidst the complex maze of characters, political ideologies, and motivations found in this novel.[55] Others find the characters themselves to be absurd and garish. Many find it difficult to plow through the meandering description of the ridiculous relationship of Stepan Trofimovich and Varvara Petrovna. In fact, almost 90 percent of the book elapses before the central event of the novel actually occurs (the murder of Shatov).

Interpreting *The Demons*

The Demons was not received warmly by the liberal and progressive press of Tsarist Russia when it was published in 1871. W. J. Leatherbarrow summarizes the feeling in writing that, "The general view was that this was a work driven by indignation rather than inspiration and that in it Dostoevsky had vilified the progressive intelligentsia by his concentration on atypical individuals."[56] Indeed, the political message of the book is unabashedly anti-progressive. By the turn of the century, a limited number of Russian thinkers turned to the novel for its mystical messages, but Soviet rule brought even this small amount of interest to an end by limiting the novel's availability.[57]

It is only with the unraveling of Soviet communism that Russian readers again turned to this novel for its seemingly prophetic message of revolution and tyranny. As Joseph Frank points out "Time and again, from 1872-1873 to the present, *The Devils [Demons]* has been attacked as a vicious slander on the Russian revolutionary movement of his day. More recently, as Russians have begun to speak freely about life in the former Soviet Union, the book has come to be seen as far more prophetic than defamatory."[58]

The novel's reception in the English-speaking world was, of course, contingent upon its translation into English.[59] Constance Garnett accomplished this in 1913 with the first of five eventual translations.[60] It was the last of his four great novels to be translated into English.

In the English-speaking world, critics differed dramatically as to how this novel should be approached. On the one hand were the critics who focused upon the metaphysical aspects of the book; on the other, those who focused upon the prophetic or political aspects of the book. A careful analysis of the notebooks used in writing the book, reveals that Dostoevsky initially constructed the novel with a metaphysical theme, only later incorporating a political theme.[61] This, no doubt, led to this critical dichotomy.[62]

There are, no doubt, metaphysical themes to be found in *The Demons*. Indeed, the primary roles of Kirillov and Shatov, as the spiritual creations of Nikolai Vsevolodovich Stavrogin, are geared toward illustrating two possible outcomes of atheism. Indeed, a great deal of space is devoted in the novel to the interaction of these three characters.

The primary focus of *The Demons*, however, is upon the political and psychological.[63] Nikolai Vsevolodovich Stavrogin is no more the primary focus of the novel than is Pyotr Stepanovich Verkhovensky. As will be seen below, it is no coincidence that the novel begins with Stepan Trofimovich Verkhovensky. He is the primary character of the book. He is the *causal force* for everything that will follow in the book. For Dostoevsky, he is the *root* of terrorism.

Indeed, in a letter that Dostoevsky sent to the future Tsar, Alexander III, he wrote,

> It's almost a historical study, in which I've sought to account for the possibility of such monstrous phenomena as the Nechaev movement occurring in our strange society. . . . Our Belinskys and Granovskys would never have believed it if they'd been told they were the direct spiritual fathers of the Nechaev band. And it's this kinship of ideas and their transmission from fathers to sons that I've tried to show in my work.[64]

This passage is absolutely pivotal in understanding the overall theme of the book, for in it we find the fundamental source through which the political and psychological roots of terrorism would flow—seemingly innocuous Western liberals such as Belinsky and Granovsky. The main character of *The Demons*, Stepan Trofimovich is carefully modeled upon the liberal Granovsky. He is the novel's main demon. Dostoevsky elaborates upon this when he explained to Maikov in October of 1870, ". . . a man who loses his people and his national roots also loses the faith of his fathers and his God. . . . Well, if you really want to know—this is the theme of my novel in essence. It's called Devils [Demons], and it describes how the devils entered into the herd of swine."[65] Once these demons have entered the swine (the people of Russia), they drown as the swine collectively jump into the water. Once the demons and their hosts have disappeared into the water, Russia is freed from demonic influences.[66]

Turgenev and the Deification of the Natural Sciences

In dealing with the generational divide between the liberal intellectuals of the 1840's and the radicals of the 1860's, Dostoevsky was revisiting a theme famously dealt with by Ivan Turgenev in his 1862 novel *Fathers and Sons*.[67] Upon publication, this novel took Russian society by storm, creating considerable controversy, and setting the parameters for the debate of social and political topics for the remainder century.[68]

The main contribution of *Fathers and Sons* to the Russian intellectual firmament lay with its introduction of the concept of "nihilism."[69] The narrative deals with the return of two young men of the 1860's who visit their fathers, who are men of the 1840's.[70] The supposed proto-type of the young men of the

1860's is a young student by the name of Yevgeny Vassilievich Bazarov who is a self-proclaimed nihilist, a character of a new type who, ". . . does not bow to any authorities; who doesn't accept any principle on faith, no matter how hallowed and venerated the principle is."[71] The novel portrays the conflicts which arise between the two generations as well as the conflicts that arise among each of the characters themselves. Turgenev masterfully presents to us how nihilism conflicts with basic human nature when he describes the failed romance between Bazarov and Ann Sergeyevna Odintsova. In the end, Turgenev portrays a nihilist with whom we can sympathize.

It is therefore predictable that the novel received a mixed reception.[72] Those on the right thought that Turgenev was either trying to flatter the young with his sympathetic view of Bazarov and those who thought he had successfully exposed the barbarism of the nihilists. Those on the left accused Turgenev of either providing those on the right with ammunition with which they could persecute the leftists or that Bazarov was a perfect model to be imitated. Caught somewhere within this debate were those who argued that the novelist himself did not know what to do with this highly ambivalent character.[73]

At first glance, it appears as though Dostoevsky falls into this last group of readers. In *The Demons*, he has the main character, Stepan Trofimovich, say this about the novel: "I don't understand Turgenev. His Bazarov is some sort of fictional character, who doesn't exist at all; they [the radicals] were the first to reject him as having no resemblance to anything. This Bazarov is some vague mixture of Nozdryov and Byron, *c'est le mot*." (10:171)

However, if we compare Bazarov with Stavrogin, the nihilist of *The Demons*, we must come to a rather different conclusion. While Bazarov merely sneaks a furtive, libertine kiss with Fenechka, Stavrogin commits a whole host of outrageous acts, the most extreme of which is the seduction of a young girl who he allows to commit suicide out of remorse for her willing sexual activities with him. If Bazarov is merely a character who professes to reject traditional ideals and morality, it is Stavrogin who actually acts upon them. It is in this light that Dostoevsky's *The Demons* appears to be, on at least one level, an attempt to reform Turgenev's soft nihilist into what he felt was a more accurate depiction of a cruel nihilist.

In focusing upon the personal qualities of Bazarov, however, we run the risk of losing the forest through the trees. The question which hangs over this novel deals more directly with the cause of this rift between fathers and sons. Even a cursory glimpse at this novel indicates that it is not with the "Belinskys and Granovskys" that we find the cause of this rift. Indeed, the character who seems most like either of these famous "Westerners" is Arkady's Uncle Pavel (Kirsanov). It is not only impossible to draw a causal link between the Arkady's Uncle Pavel and Bazarov, but the two actually end up fighting a duel. Bazarov disapproves of the Western habits of Pavel as much as Pavel hates the nihilism of Bazarov. Turgenev is clearly trying to clear the "Westerners" like Belinsky and Granovsky for any sort of blame in the creation of Bazarov the nihilist.

For Turgenev, the source of Bazarov's nihilism is science. By not bowing to any authority and not accepting any principle on faith he is espousing scientific empiricism. He studies natural science in University and aspires to be a doctor. Toward the beginning of the novel he explains that he sees no difference between frogs and humans. He states, "I'm going to split the frog open to see what's going on inside of him; since you and I are no different from frogs, except that we walk on our hind legs, I'll find out what's happening inside of us too."[74] When Uncle Pavel complains that Bazarov believes in frogs, but not in principles he is only getting it partially correct. Bazarov actually believes in the principle of science.

Science claims to be about facts not values or ideals. As a scientist, Bazarov disapproves of Pushkin, Russia's national poet, because, "A passable chemist is twenty times as useful as any kind of poet."[75] He also claims that, ". . . Raphael's not worth a cent . . ."[76] and that, "Nature isn't a temple, but a workshop, in which man is a worker."[77]

For Bazarov, science has become his belief-system—his God. It is an empirical God without ideals. Lacking ideals not only means that there is no good and evil, but that any sentiment which requires ideals is in conflict with this new God. This, of course, precludes love.

Bazarov's crisis occurs when he falls in love with Anna Sergeyevna Odintsova. He tries to explain his love in scientific terms by describing her physically. He states, "What a generous body! . . . If it were only in the dissecting room right now!"[78] This attempt to explain his attraction in a scientific manner does not quell his confusion over being in love with her.

Odintsova's rejection of Bazarov is devastating for him. Although he can not rationalize his feelings scientifically, he concludes that without her love he has no reason to live. He becomes a "self-destroyer."[79] It is no irony that the method by which Bazarov destroys himself is science; he cuts himself while conducting a seemingly needless autopsy on a man who had died of typhus. He not only does not take the appropriate precautions in conducting this procedure, but after being cut, does not cauterize the wound immediately.

Love can not be scientifically explained, it can not be measured or observed. After Odintsova rejects his overtures, Bazarov tells Odintsova, ". . . And then love . . . is just an imaginary feeling."[80] Odintsova responds, "Really? I'm delighted to hear that."[81] She does not seem convinced however and follows up with this topic later in the story, now in the form of a question to the betrothed Katya and Arkady. She asks, "Children! . . . is it true that love's an imaginary feeling?"[82]

Turgenev powerfully ends the novel with an answer to this question. There is nothing imaginary about the love Bazarov's parents feel toward their only child. Turgenev describes the grave of Bazarov by writing, "It is often visited by two now very old people from the little village near by—a man with his wife. Leaning on one another they come, walking with heavy steps; they go up to the fence, fall on their knees, and kneeling, cry endlessly and bitterly, and look endlessly and intensely at the mute stone under which lies their son."[83]

Bazarov deifies science to his last breath. As he lay dying, Bazarov's father asks him to do his "Christian duty" and receive last rites. He asks to wait, assuring his father that this can be done even to those who are unconscious. Indeed, Bazarov is unconscious when final rites are finally performed. Turgenev writes, "When he was given extreme unction, when the holy oil touched his chest, one of his eyes opened, and it seemed as if at the sight of the priest in his vestments, the smoking censers, the taper in front of the image—something like a shudder of horror was momentarily reflected on his livid face."[84]

For Turgenev, an individual who makes a God out of science is in essence a nihilist. Not only does such deification result in the unhappiness of Bazarov and Odintsova, but in the former's death. Science flies in the face of human nature and of love and of happiness. For Turgenev, love is a basic human requirement. As we shall see, this fundamental message of *Fathers and Sons* is very much in keeping with the fundamental message of *The Demons*. Strangely, the two great thinkers were at odds throughout most of their lives. Indeed, Dostoevsky once famously claimed that Turgenev was a renegade Russian and, ". . . advised him to procure a telescope which might enable him to see Russia a little better" from his home in Germany.[85]

It is important to remember, however, that this conflict was not ideological, but personal.[86] At the very core of the rivalry between Dostoevsky and Turgenev was a class distinction felt quite acutely by Dostoevsky. Hints of this are seen in his description of their very first meeting, which occurred at the end of 1845. In a letter describing the event, he wrote:

> Recently the poet Turgenev came back from Paris . . . and he attached himself to me at first sight with such devotion that Belinsky explains it by saying he has fallen in love with me! . . . I have all but fallen in love with him myself. A poet, an aristocrat, talented, handsome, rich, intelligent, well-educated, and twenty-five years old. And, to conclude, a noble character, infinitely direct and open, formed in a good school.[87]

Trouble between the two occurred fairly quickly. A witness to their first few meetings wrote that Dostoevsky was clearly uncomfortable and shy at the time he met Turgenev (which occurred as they both participated in literary activities managed by Belinsky). Once he had become used to his new acquaintances and surroundings, his behavior changed. She writes, "Because of his youth and nervousness . . . he did not know how to conduct himself, and he would only too clearly express his conceit as an author and his high opinion of his own literary talent."[88] The other members of the literary circle, including Turgenev, retaliated against him by ridiculing him, an activity which culminated in a satirical poem, written at the end of 1846 by Turgenev and Nekrasov, which labeled Dostoevsky as a "pimple" on the face of literature.[89]

It is within this context that we should read Dostoevsky's return volley in the form of the character of Karmazinov in *The Demons*. In this lampoon of Turgenev, Dostoevsky describes a once-has-been writer, ". . . of the average sort, who are usually taken almost for geniuses in their lifetime, not only vanish from people's memory almost without trace and somehow suddenly when they die, but it happens that even in their lifetime, as soon as a new generation grows up to replace the one in whose time they were active—they are forgotten and disregarded by everyone inconceivably quickly." (10:69)

The most obvious characteristic about Karmazinov that we must note is his excessive vanity and triteness. This is a vanity which, according the novel's narrator, ". . . sometimes take on proportions worthy of wonder. . . ." (10:69) Toward the end of the novel, Karmazinov arranges a little skit to be performed at the fete. The narrator reminds us, "It would be hard to imagine a more pathetic, trite, giftless, and insipid allegory than this 'quadrille of literature.'" (10:389)

It is not just Turgenev's perceived vanity that bothered Dostoevsky, but his lack of rootedness in Russia. Dostoevsky felt that nothing illustrates an individual's connection to a place so clearly as the choice he makes for his own final resting place.[90] In *The Demons*, Dostoevsky makes clear that Karmazinov wants to be laid to rest abroad. Karmazinov states in his final speech to the fete, "Yes, it will be my farewell; I'll say my Merci and leave, and there . . . in Karlsruhe . . . . I shall close my eyes. . . ." (10:350)

Dostoevsky was also bothered by the fact that he perceived that Turgenev was pandering to the younger generation—backing away from positions that the two had agreed upon earlier. He portrays Karmazinov/Turgenev as someone who simply lives for the approval of others that occupy the same cosmopolitan world. The narrator reminds us, "Mr. Karmazinov most certainly had in mind his relations with the progressive young men of both capitals. The great writer trembled morbidly before the newest revolutionary young men, and, imagining in his ignorance of the matter that the keys to the Russian future were in their hands, sucked up to them humiliatingly, the more so since they paid no attention at all to him." (10:170) He would even sell his soul for such approval, "It was said of Karmazinov that he valued his connections with influential people and with higher society almost more than his soul." (10:69)

Why is this important? Dostoevsky resented and envied Turgenev's wealth, fame, and social grace. To put it another way, he resented Turgenev's cosmopolitan refinement. In a sadly predictable manner, Dostoevsky's reaction to Turgenev was what one would expect from any similar encounter between a country rustic and an urban sophisticate. As we shall shortly see, this sensitivity enabled Dostoevsky to understand this commonplace psychological phenomenon better than most.

None of this should blind us, however, to their general agreement about those things harmful to Russian society. As we shall shortly see, they both ultimately agreed on the dangers of a deified science. What is sometimes astounding to modern readers is that the great contemporary of both Turgenev and Dostoevsky agreed with this—Leo Tolstoy.

Tolstoy and the Deification of the Social Sciences

Isaiah Berlin once famously wrote that intellectuals can be classified as either hedgehogs or foxes. The former are thinkers who relate everything to a single central vision or universal organizing principle, while the latter pursue ideas which are scattered, diverse, and even contradictory. In this sense, the hedgehogs are centripetal in their thinking; the foxes are centrifugal. Dostoevsky, like Dante, Plato, Lucretius, Pascal, Hegel, Nietzsche, Ibsen, and Proust, was a hedgehog. Shakespeare, Herodotus, Aristotle, Montaigne, Erasmus, Molière, Goethe, Pushkin, Balzak, and Joyce were foxes. Berlin then explains, "Indeed, it would not be absurd to say that Russian literature is spanned by these gigantic figures—at one pole Pushkin [an arch-fox], at the other Dostoevsky [an arch-hedgehog]; and that the characteristic of other Russian writers can, by those who find it useful or enjoyable to ask that kind of question, to some degree be determined in relation to these great opposites."[91]

The focus of Berlin's famous essay, however, is upon Tolstoy and his philosophy of history found in his great novel *War and Peace*. Although so much can be found in this novel, it is Tolstoy's philosophy of history that is the "universal organizing principle" of the book. Although Berlin considered Tolstoy to be a fox, it is this "universal organizing principle" which makes him a hedgehog.

While Turgenev was concerned that the deification of science results in moral nihilism, Tolstoy was concerned that such a deification results in error in human reason. Tolstoy nicely sums this up at the beginning of book eleven of *War and Peace* when he writes,

> For human reason, absolute continuity of movement is incomprehensible. Man begins to understand the laws of any kind of movement only when he examines the arbitrarily chosen units of that movement. But at the same time it is from this arbitrary division of continuous movement into discrete units that the greater part of human errors proceeds.[92]

Tolstoy argues that this concern is not a new one. He recalls that the ancient Greeks were quite aware of the errors that could result in the scientific process of parsing the whole, and provides a brief description of Zeno's Paradox. In this illustration, one is encouraged to imagine a race between the legendary Achilles and a tortoise. In order for human reason to comprehend how the race will proceed, Zeno parses it down into small time segments. He points out that because Achilles is ten times as fast as the tortoise, the latter is given an advantage of ten units. Once the race has begun, measurements are taken each time Achilles reaches the point where the tortoise was at the end of the preceding time segment. The result is that Achilles always comes closer to closing the gap between himself and the tortoise, but never quite catches him.

In this way, the parsing of the whole leads to an error in human reason.[93] It is certainly not conceivable to the historian who attempts to understand the "laws of historical movement." The only means by which an historian can understand such laws is by accepting that an "infinitesimal unit of observation" must be taken into account, within the context of an infinite number of such observations. Of course, such a thing can not be done. What can be done, however, is the conceptualization of the "uniform strivings of people" as the sum of the infinite number of infinitesimal events surrounding any particular event.[94]

The application of science to the understanding of human history is not the only type of error which can occur. A "science" of military strategy can be equally as erroneous in outcome. Tolstoy clarifies how he feels about the introduction of this new science in Russia when he writes,

> Pfuel [a German General] was one of those hopelessly, permanently, painfully self-assured men as only Germans can be, and precisely because only Germans can be self-assured on the basis of an abstract idea—science, that is, an imaginary knowledge of the perfect truth. A Frenchman is self-assured because he considers himself personally, in mind as well as body, irresistibly enchanting for men as well as women. An Englishman is self-assured on the grounds that he is a citizen of the best-organized state in the world, and therefore, as an Englishman, he always knows what he must do, and knows that everything he does as an Englishman is unquestionably good. An Italian is self-assured because he is excitable and easily forgets himself and others. A Russian is self-assured precisely because he does not know anything and does not want to know anything, because he does not believe it possible to know anything fully. A German is self-assured worst of all, and most firmly of all, and most disgustingly of all, because he imagines that he knows the truth, science, which he has invented himself, but which for him is the absolute truth.[95]

For Tolstoy strategy can not understand the outcome of a battle by analyzing the isolated portions of it (leadership, deployment of troops, armament, etc.). In essence, military leaders who rely upon the science of strategy commit the error of Zeno's paradox.

Like Turgenev, Tolstoy also understood that science can not deal with those phenomena which can not be measured or observed. He does this most notably in the figure of Napoleon who is a clever tactician, but does not understand issues of "spirit." This is seen most clearly in Napoleon's speech upon first seeing Moscow. He states, "I will give them [the Russians] the laws of justice, I will show them the meaning of true civilization; I will make the generation of boyars remember the name of their conqueror with love."[96] This statement is as ridiculous as saying that Achilles will never pass the tortoise. A conquered people do not love a cruel, murderous oppressor; they fear him.

The deification of science destroys ideals. Science never claims to be about ideals—it is empirical and objective. As such, it has displaced the ideals of the three moral pillars of Western civilization. Tolstoy explains,

> In the place of the former god-pleasing goals of the peoples—the Jews, the Greeks, the Romans—which the ancients took for the goals of the movement of mankind, modern history has set up its own goals—the good of the French, the Germans, the English, and, in its highest abstraction, the goal of the good of all human civilization, usually understood as the people occupying the small northwest corner of a large continent. . . . Modern history has rejected the beliefs of the ancients without putting in their place a new view. . . .[97]

To state it differently, modern science has killed the Gods of the Jewish, Greek, and Roman nations and replaced them with the Gods of the French, German, and English peoples. Who, or what, are these new Gods? As we read above, the people of these nations are self-confident because they feel they know the Truth, which is their God. As Tolstoy told us earlier, the Germans are self-confident because they know the absolute truth—science. The French, as individuals who are "irresistibly attractive to men and women alike," have deified themselves. The English, who are self-confident because they know they are from the best-organized state in the world, have deified the politics and economics of their own country (liberalism and free markets).

The Solution of the Fist

As Tolstoy was writing *War and Peace*, Dostoevsky was contemplating the very same thoughts. Shortly after Tolstoy completed this novel, Dostoevsky wrote the following passage in *The Demons*:

> The Jews lived only to await the arrival of the true God and left to the world the true God. The Greeks deified nature and bequeathed the world their religion, that is, philosophy and art. Rome deified the people in the State, and bequeathed the idea of the State to the nations. France throughout her long history was only the incarnation and development of the Roman god, and if they have at last flung their Roman god into the abyss and plunged into atheism, which, for the time being, they call socialism, it is solely because socialism is, at any rate, healthier than Roman Catholicism. (10:197)

It is fascinating that both Tolstoy and Dostoevsky saw the Jews, Greeks, and Romans as the three moral pillars of Western civilization. For both of them, each bequeathed to civilization their ideals—their Gods. The Jews bequeath to the world a divine God (adopted by Christianity), the Greeks contributed their ideals of philosophy and art, and the Romans imparted their ideals of civic virtue (duty, honor, citizenship, patriotism, and loyalty).

In their writings, Turgenev and Tolstoy are primarily focused upon the death of the Jewish and Greek Gods at the hands of (German) science. The Roman God, the God overlooked by both of them, is notably a political God. This is where Dostoevsky fills the gap in his most political of novels, *The Demons*. For him, the Jewish, Greek, and Roman Gods are all threatened by the modern

Gods. For Dostoevsky, the force behind these three modern Gods is the Deification of Reason.

As already mentioned, Dostoevsky differed from Turgenev and Tolstoy in what he felt would be the end result of the death of the ancient Gods. He felt that such a circumstance would result in nihilistic violence. This is precisely what he has Shatov say in his speech to Stavrogin,

> Never has reason ever had the power to define good and evil, nor even to distinguish between good and evil, even approximately; on the contrary, it has always mixed them up in a shameful and pitiful way; science has even given the solution of the fist. (10:199)

For Dostoevsky the "solution of the fist" is the political side of reason and science. It is a politics which is tyrannical in goal and terroristic in method. As we shall see, Dostoevsky's goal in *The Demons* is to demonstrate that the God of Reason, having displaced the Ancient Gods, creates the amoral psychological conditions for terroristic violence and the political conditions for tyranny.

This deification of reason is what Dostoevsky felt was happening in the West. The West had rejected the ancient Gods for science and reason. In so doing, it created an amoral world—a nihilistic world. Dostoevsky was not alone, however, in thinking that the Deification of Reason could have catastrophic social and political results. In fact, Dostoevsky was engaging in a dialogue with other great thinkers about this critical question. As we just saw, at home, this dialogue was conducted with Turgenev and Tolstoy. As we shall see shortly, he also directly engaged two Western thinkers in *The Demons*: Jean-Jacques Rousseau and Alexis de Tocqueville. Without an adequate understanding of how he engaged these writers, a complete understanding of his writings is impossible.

Modernity and Terrorism

If we are to accept that terrorism is a modern phenomenon in the West, it is difficult to ignore the concerns of Turgenev, Tolstoy, and Dostoevsky who observed the sudden and dramatic advent of modernity in Russia. Turgenev's fear of the deification of natural science and the subsequent demoralization of human behavior was a clear dilemma for Russia of the nineteenth century. Few today can deny that science claims to be "amoral." Science is about the "what is" not the "what should be." If a value-less science is to provide for the ideals of a society, then the only thing that can follow is societal-level nihilism. Clearly, this is problematic.

Turgenev's novel opens the entire moral dimension of terrorism. His work forces us to consider such questions as: can the death of an innocent child be a justifiable price in the pursuit of political change? His ideas would imply that science can address the "effectiveness" of terrorism as a political strategy, but it can not address the moral dimensions.

Tolstoy's contention that the deification of science can lead to erroneous reasoning is also difficult to ignore. Not only does the scientific parsing of reality lead to the potential for a skewed understanding of reality, but science can not grapple with those issues which can not be measured or observed. Surely, we as social scientists in our attempt to understand terrorism are guilty of these things as well. We create narrow hypotheses to be tested, the end result of which is that we still know nothing about terrorism and its causes.

Tolstoy also warns of the dangers of ignoring those elements of reality that can not be measured or observed. Rarely do social scientists talk about the "rage" or "humiliation" of terrorists. It is within this context that Thomas Friedman writes, "The single most underappreciated force in international relations is humiliation."[98] It is underappreciated because it can not be measured or quantified. We can not really "prove" that it exists in any particular circumstance. As it can not be "proved," we erroneously conclude that it must not exist.

Dostoevsky's explanation is the fullest. He looks to the modern deification of Reason as the source of terroristic violence and tyranny. In abandoning the ancient sources of morality, the ancient Gods, and replacing them with the modern Gods of atheism, science, and liberalism, we have abandoned any sort of moral constraint that helped to keep violence and tyranny in check. His explanation, however, is subtle. He employs impeccable logic in the unfolding of the complex web of political and psychological evolution. Importantly, in discussing this, he directly addresses those thinkers who shared his concerns about the "Age of Reason." Let us now take a look at these.

Notes

1. Norman M. Naimark, "Terrorism and the Fall of Imperial Russia," *Terrorism and Political Violence* 2, No. 2 (Summer 1990): 174.

2. Naimark, "Terrorism and the Fall of Imperial Russia," 174.

3. Naimark, "Terrorism and the Fall of Imperial Russia," 174.

4. Sergey Nechaev, "Catechism of the Revolutionist (1869)," in Walter Laqueur, ed., *Voices of Terror: Manifestos, Writings and Manuals of Al Qaeda, Hamas, and Other Terrorists from Around the World and Throughout the Ages* (New York: Reed Press, 2004): 71.

5. Bruce Hoffman, *Inside Terrorism* (New York: Columbia University Press, 1998): 29-38.

6. Andrew Silke writes, "Our knowledge of terrorism most certainly is deficient but the field shows no clear ability to improve this situation. After thirty years of study, we simply should know more about terrorism than we currently do. That we continue to languish at this level of ignorance on such a serious subject is a cause of grave concern." See Andrew Silke, "The Devil You Know: Continuing Problems with Research on Terrorism," *Terrorism and Political Violence* 13 (Winter 2001): 13.

7. The most serious attempt to debunk the link between modernity (specifically modern technology) and terrorism was seen in 1984 in an article written by David

Rapoport in which he examined three pre-modern "terrorist" groups, the Thugs, the Assassins, and the Zealots. By his own admission, these three groups were "holy terrorists"—not motivated by a political cause (which is a fundamental quality of terrorists today). See David C. Rapoport, "Terrorism in Three Religious Traditions, *The American Political Science Review* 78, No. 3 (September 1984): 658-677.

8. For a detailed discussion of the difficulties associated with defining terrorism see: Bruce Hoffman, *Inside Terrorism* (New York: Columbia University Press, 1998): 13-44.

9. Dave Grossman, *On Killing: The Psychological Cost of Learning to Kill in War and Society* (Boston: Little, Brown and Company, 1995): 3.

10. Dave Grossman, *On Killing*, 4.

11. Dave Grossman, *On Killing*, 4.

12. Marcus E. Ethridge, *The Political Research Experience: Readings and Analysis* (Armonk, New York : M. E. Sharpe, 1990): 2.

13. Two books are noteworthy in discussing the need to deal with values and belief systems of political movements: David M. Ricci, *The Tragedy of Political Science* (New Haven, Conn.: Yale University Press, 1984) and Allan Bloom, *The Closing of the American Mind* (New York: Simon & Schuster, 1987).

14. Most agree that the term itself is highly derogatory—an aspersion to be cast at one's enemies. Indeed, those that engage in terrorist activities insist that they are not terrorists, referring to themselves with terms which cloak the negative associations of killing *innocent* people in the name of a political idea: The Irish Republican *Army*, The Red *Brigades*, The Shining Path. See Bruce Hoffman, *Inside Terrorism* (New York: Columbia University Press, 1998).

15. Bruce Hoffman, *Inside Terrorism*, 43.

16. The two finest books on the evolution of nationalism are: Ernest Gellner, *Nations and Nationalism* (Ithaca, New York: Cornell University Press, 1983) and Benedict Anderson, *Imagined Communities: Reflections on the Origin and Spread of Nationalism* (New York: Verso, 1983).

17. Some will argue that "narcoterrorism" represents yet another form of terrorism. However, a narcoterrorist group like Colombia's FARC operates almost exclusively with a profit-making goal—a very non-political activity. Other narcoterrorist groups are similar thereby not meeting the commonly accepted requirement that a terrorist group should have a political goal.

18. Benedict Anderson, *Imagined Communities: Reflections on the Origin and Spread of Nationalism*, 58.

19. Osama bin Laden, "Jihad Against Jews and Crusaders," in Walter Laqueur, ed., *Voices of Terror: Manifestos, Writings and Manuals of Al Qaeda, Hamas, and Other Terrorists from Around the World and Throughout the Ages* (New York: Reed Press, 2004): 410-412.

20. An excellent summary of Al-Qaeda's background and motivations can be found in Daniel Byman, "Al-Qaeda As An Adversary: Do We Understand Our Enemy?" *World Politics* 56 (October 2003): 139-163.

21. Retrieved from http://www.animalliberationpressoffice.org/history.htm (7 October 2008).

22. Siamak Khatami, "Between Class and Nation: Ideology and Radical Basque Ethnonationalism," *Studies in Conflict and Terrorism*, 20 (1997): 395-417.

23. This is only an approximate periodization. Jacques Barzun provides a much more accurate one in which he writes, ". . . the period–1500-1660–was dominated by the issue of what to believe in religion; the second–1661-1789–by what to do about the status

of the individual and the mode of government; the third–1790-1920–by what means to achieve social and economic equality." See Jacques Barzun, *From Dawn to Decadence: 1500 to the Present* (New York: HarperCollins, 2000): xxi.

24. The title of Dostoevsky's novel, *Besy*, has been translated in three different ways: *The Possessed*, *The Devils*, and *The Demons*. Here we will refer to it as *The Demons*.

25. Reference notes here are to F. M. Dostoevskij, *Besy*, Vol 10 and 11 (Leningrad: Izdatel'stvo "Nauka," 1974). Ultimately, I am responsible for the translation from Russian to English although I am heavily indebted to two previous translations that I found to be enormously helpful in this task: Fyodor Dostoevsky, *Demons*, trans. Richard Pevear and Larissa Volokhonsky (New York: Vintage Books, 1994) and Fyodor Dostoevsky, *Devils*, trans. Michael Katz (New York: Oxford University Press, 1992).

26. See Richard Curle, *Characters of Dostoevsky: Studies from Four Novels* (New York: Russell & Russell, 1966), title page.

27. This Freudian quote is attributed to Edward Wasiolek. See Richard Pope and Judy Turner, "Toward Understanding Stavrogin," *Slavic Review* 49 (Winter 1990): 543-553.

28. For a survey of the work available today on terrorist motivations see Gordon H. McCormick, "Terrorist Decision Making," *Annual Review of Political Science* 6 (2003): 491-492. For a somewhat different breakdown see Rex A. Hudson, *The Sociology and Psychology of Terrorism: Who Becomes a Terrorist and Why?* (Guilford, Conn.: Lyons Press, 1999).

29. Gordon H. McCormick, "Terrorist Decision Making," 491.

30. Martha Crenshaw, "The Causes of Terrorism." *Comparative Politics* 13 (July 1981): 390. See also Bruce Hoffman, *Inside Terrorism* (New York: Columbia University Press, 1998): 7.

31. Robert A. Pape, "The Strategic Logic of Suicide Terrorism," *American Political Science Review* 97 (August 2003): 343-361.

32. Gordon H. McCormick, "Terrorist Decision Making," *Annual Review of Political Science* 6 (2003): 492.

33. Gordon H. McCormick, "Terrorist Decision Making," 492.

34. Ehud Sprinzak, "The Process of Delegitimization: Towards a Linkage Theory of Political Terrorism," *Terrorism Political Violence* 3 (1991): 51. For more on this see, Ehud Sprinzak, "The Psychological Formation of Extreme Left Terrorism in a Democracy," in *Origins of Terrorism: Psychologies, Ideologies, Theologies, States of Mind*, Walter Reich, ed. (Washington, D.C.: Woodrow Wilson Press, 1998): 65-85.

35. For a classic statement on this approach see Ted R. Gurr, *Why Men Rebel* (Princeton, New Jersey: Princeton University Press, 1971).

36. Jerrold M. Post, "Terrorist Psycho-logic: Terrorist Behavior as a Product of Psychological Forces," in Walter Reich, ed., *Origins of Terrorism: Psychologies, Ideologies, Theologies, States of Mind* (Washington, D.C.: Woodrow Wilson Center Press, 1998): 25.

37. Jerrold M. Post, "Terrorist Psycho-logic: Terrorist Behavior as a Product of Psychological Forces," 27.

38. Jerrold M. Post, "Terrorist Psycho-logic: Terrorist Behavior as a Product of Psychological Forces," 28.

39. Jerrold M. Post, "Terrorist Psycho-logic: Terrorist Behavior as a Product of Psychological Forces," 28.

40. James Gilligan, "Shame, Guilt, and Violence," *Social Research* 70, no. 4 (Winter 2003): 1149-1181.

41. James Gilligan, "Shame, Guilt, and Violence," 1151.

42. James Gilligan, "Shame, Guilt, and Violence," 1153.

43. James Gilligan, "Shame, Guilt, and Violence," 1154.

44. James Gilligan, "Shame, Guilt, and Violence," 1153.

45. James Gilligan, "Shame, Guilt, and Violence," 1163.

46. James Gilligan, "Shame, Guilt, and Violence," 1152.

47. James Gilligan, "Shame, Guilt, and Violence," 1152.

48. Walter Laqueur, *The New Terrorism: Fanaticism and the Arms of Mass Destruction* (New York: Oxford University Press, 1999): 102.

49. The use of literature is very much in keeping with the sentiments of David Ricci who has written, "Political science's tragic condition indicates a need for practitioners to search out wisdom via renewed dedication to continuing a great conversation embodied in great books old and new." David Ricci, *The Tragedy of Political Science* (New Haven, Conn.: Yale University Press, 1984): 315. See also Catherine Zuckert, "Why Political Scientists Want to Study Literature," *PS: Political Science & Politics* (June 1995).

50. Joseph Frank, *Dostoevsky: The Miraculous Years, 1865-1871* (Princeton, New Jersey: Princeton University Press, 1995)

51. Joseph Frank, *Dostoevsky: The Miraculous Years, 1865-1871*, 465-466.

52. There are, of course, a large number of characters appearing and disappearing throughout the novel. None, however, are more important to the overall messages of the novel than these four.

53. Upon initial inspection, a reader is tempted to conclude that Stavrogin's behavior toward women in the novel is driven subconsciously by a psychological attempt to exact revenge upon all women for the maternal neglect he experienced as a child.

54. Not only does Pyotr Stepanovich follow Nikolai Vsevolodovich's suggestion, but he adopts this very same strategy in trying to cement him to the group by killing his "secret" wife in such a way that it would look like he did it. Pyotr Stepanovich succeeds in killing this woman (and her brother) and burning down a good portion of the town. He does not succeed in cementing Nikolai Vsevolodovich to the group.

55. In considering *The Demons*, Vladimir Nabokov has written, "Considered as novels, his works fall to pieces; considered as plays, they are much too long, diffuse, and badly balanced," in Vladimir Nabokov, *Lectures on Russian Literature* (New York: Harcourt Brace & Company, 1981): 130.

56. W. J. Leatherbarrow, ed., *Dostoevsky's* The Devils: *A Critical Companion* (Evanston, Ill.: Northwestern University Press, 1999): 55.

57. Throughout the Soviet period, the novel was available only in the official academic edition as Volumes 10 and 11. W. J. Leatherbarrow, ed., *Dostoevsky's* The Devils: *A Critical Companion*, 55.

58. Joseph Frank, *Dostoevsky: The Miraculous Years, 1865-1871*, 438.

59. As Helen Muchnic reminds us, Dostoevsky's novels were received in translation, "with almost unanimous approbation." Helen Muchnic, *Dostoevsky's English Reputation* (New York: Octagon Books, 1969): 68.

60. See Fyodor Dostoyevsky, *The Possessed: A Novel in Three parts* (New York: Macmillan Company, 1913).

61. While the notebooks can have some utility in helping to understand Dostoevsky's intentions, I have chosen to focus on that which he actually decided to say rather than what he might have intended to say as seen in the notebooks.

62. For a metaphysical approach see the first full-length critical book written in English on Dostoevsky: J. Middleton Murry, *Fyodor Dostoevsky: A Critical Study* (New York: Russell & Russell, 1966): v. Another classic example of the metaphysical approach can be found in Derek Traversi, *"Dostoevsky,"* in Rene Wellek, ed, *Dostoevsky: A Collection of Critical Essays* (Englewood Cliffs, New Jersey: Prentice-Hall, 1962). A classic example of the political approach can be found with Irving Howe, "Dostoevsky: The Politics of Salvation," in Rene Wellek, ed., *Dostoevsky: A Collection of Critical Essays* (Englewood Cliffs, New Jersey: Prentice Hall, 1962): 53-70.

63. James Billington, the long-time Librarian of Congress, states that it is among the five most important books ever written. He states, "It describes terrorism before terrorism even existed. The best political novel ever written." See: "A Life in Books," *Newsweek* (February 5, 2007): 18.

64. These words of Dostoevsky are provided by Michael R. Katz on page ix in his Introduction to his translation of this novel. See Michael R. Katz, "Introduction," in Fyodor Dostoevsky, *Devils*, trans. Michael R. Katz (Oxford: Oxford University Press, 1992).

65. Michael R. Katz, "Introduction," xii.

66. As we shall see, Dostoevsky borrows this analogy from Luke 8:32-35.

67. The title of this novel is commonly translated as, *Fathers and Sons* although a more precise translation would be *Fathers and Children.*

68. Joseph Frank, *Dostoevsky: The Stir of Liberation, 1860-1865,* 163.

69. Joseph Frank, *Dostoevsky: The Stir of Liberation, 1860-1865,* 170.

70. For Turgenev, mothers play a minor role in the description of this generation divide.

71. Ivan Turgenev, *Fathers and Sons,* trans. Barbara Makanowitzky (New York: Bantam Books, 1981): 20.

72. As Isaiah Berlin so accurately noted, "In the violent babel of voices aroused by the novel, at least five attitudes can be distinguished." See Isaiah Berlin "Fathers and Children, the Romanes Lecture 1970," 36 in Ivan S. Turgenev, *Fathers and Sons,* trans. Rosemary Edmonds (New York: Penguin, 1985): 7-58.

73. Isaiah Berlin "Fathers and Children, the Romanes Lecture 1970."

74. Ivan Turgenev, *Fathers and Sons*, 16.

75. Ivan Turgenev, *Fathers and Sons*, 23.

76. Ivan Turgenev, *Fathers and Sons*, 51.

77. Ivan Turgenev, *Fathers and Sons*, 40.

78. Ivan Turgenev, *Fathers and Sons*, 76.

79. Ivan Turgenev, *Fathers and Sons*, 125.

80. Ivan Turgenev, *Fathers and Sons*, 172.

81. Ivan Turgenev, *Fathers and Sons*, 172.

82. Ivan Turgenev, *Fathers and Sons*, 182.

83. Ivan Turgenev, *Fathers and Sons*, 203.

84. Ivan Turgenev, *Fathers and Sons*, 198.

85. Isaiah Berlin "Fathers and Children, the Romanes Lecture 1970," 41.

86. Donna Tussing Orwin, *Consequences of Consciousness: Turgenev, Dostoevsky, and Tolstoy* (Stanford, California: Stanford University Press, 2007).

87. Joseph Frank, *Dostoevsky: The Seeds of Revolt, 1821-1849* (Princeton, New Jersey: Princeton University Press, 1979): 162.

88. Joseph Frank, *Dostoevsky: The Seeds of Revolt, 1821-1849,* 163.

89. Joseph Frank, *Dostoevsky: The Seeds of Revolt, 1821-1849,* 168.

90. This was probably unfair of Dostoevsky. While Turgenev did die in Paris, he was buried, according to his wishes, in St. Petersburg.

91. Isaiah Berlin, *The Hedgehog and the Fox: An Essay on Tolstoy's View of History* (London: George Weidenfeld & Nicolson Limited, 1988): 4.

92. Leo Tolstoy, *War and Peace*, trans. Richard Pevear and Larissa Volokhonsky (New York: Alfred A. Knopf, 2007): 821.

93. He admits that modern mathematics has solved this paradox by allowing for infinitesimal quantities to be dealt with. He thus must grant that it is theoretically possible to understand the whole through a process of examining the infinitesimal parts. See Leo Tolstoy, *War and Peace,* 821.

94. Leo Tolstoy, *War and Peace,* 822.

95. Leo Tolstoy, *War and Peace,* 639.

96. Leo Tolstoy, *War and Peace,* 872.

97. Leo Tolstoy, *War and Peace,* 1179.

98. James Gilligan, "Shame, Guilt, and Violence," 1163.

Chapter 2
Cosmopolitanism and Its Discontents

It is not often recognized that the modern culture we read about in our tabloids and magazines finds its roots in the cosmopolitan revolution of eighteenth century Paris. When we read Rousseau's accounts of life there, the culture of youth, the bourgeois urbanity, the hyper-materialism, the domination of frivolous entertainment (and the glorification of those who provide it), the collapse of marriage and of modesty and of deeply felt sentiments, we could just as well be reading about twentieth century Los Angeles.

It is, of course, easy to denounce the frivolous, plastic culture of Los Angeles; it is much harder to write off the political ideas and modes of inquiry that emerged from the minds of the Parisian enlightenment thinkers. After all, it is here that we find individuals who took the concepts of political freedom and equality quite seriously. It is here that we find efforts to understand the common bond of humanity that could potentially unite nations. It is here that we find the emergence of rational, scientific analysis, and its application to natural and social relationships.

Any effort to understand Dostoevsky's writings must begin with an understanding of the cultural aspects of cosmopolitanism. In fact, two of the four great novels produced by Dostoevsky—*The Idiot* and *The Demons*—are primarily focused upon the denunciation of the cosmopolitan ethos. In *The Idiot*, Dostoevsky presents us with a "beautiful soul," a noble savage of genuine sentiments, who can not withstand the pressures of cosmopolitan society, and who, in the end, causes more difficulties than he resolves. In *The Demons*, we see how cosmopolitan ideas metastasize and create a nihilistic generation responsible for the first wave of terrorism in Western history. In both novels it is cosmopolitan culture that is ultimately responsible for ruining the lives of those that it touches.

One of the keenest observers of cosmopolitanism was Jean-Jacques Rousseau, who had the distinct advantage of observing it at its birth. In his book, *Julie, or the New Heloise* (hereafter referred to as *La Nouvelle Heloise*), Rousseau describes better than any other observer, before or since, cosmopolitan culture and its effects upon the way in which cosmopolitans think, feel, and behave. He also describes how this culture leads to the destruction of human happiness.

As we shall see, Dostoevsky was clearly influenced by *La Nouvelle Heloise*. His first novel, *Poor People* (1847), was written in the epistolary form, a style then out of fashion, but which had been made famous to French readers by *La Nouvelle Heloise*.[1] In *The Idiot*, Rousseau's Switzerland is the starting and ending point for the main character, Lev Myshkin. In *The Demons*, Vevey, Switzerland is the starting point for Nikolai Vsevolodovich's romances with Lizaveta Nikolaevna and Darya Pavlovna—the same exact town in which Rousseau's two lovers began their love affair in *La Nouvelle Heloise*. The rustic and alpine Swiss canton of Uri is the (suggested) ending point for Nikolai Vsevolodovich as well. In both *The Idiot* and *The Demons*, Rousseau is mentioned by name (one time each). Perhaps most importantly, the theme of both novels—how the artificiality of cosmopolitan society ruins the lives of those living within it—is one and the same.[2]

What has heretofore not been recognized by scholars is that *La Nouvelle Heloise* is central to Dostoevsky's thought in that it isolates the key cultural phenomenon (at least for Dostoevsky) that threatened Russia—the displacement of local (Russian) culture with cosmopolitan culture. In *The Idiot* and *The Demons* he puts into prose what Rousseau described in letters about cosmopolitan life. Both writers were clearly disapproving. Dostoevsky's solution, however, is so dramatically different that these two novels can not be considered as anything but a direct rebuttal to *La Nouvelle Heloise*.

The first step we must take in understanding Dostoevsky involves exploring how he understood the concept of love. Indeed, his primary goal in *The Idiot* was to correct Rousseau, whose image of love had been popularized in *La Nouvelle Heloise*. Dostoevsky's approach, however, is far too sublime to simply state that the opposite of what is wrong must be right. In *The Idiot*, Dostoevsky gives us a character devoted to a Rousseauean (erotic) love who meets a most unfortunate fate. However, he also gives us a man devoted to a purely charitable form of love, whose purity can not save him from the artifices of cosmopolitan society. For Dostoevsky, neither man had it completely right; for him, the correct understanding of romantic love involves an amalgamation of both erotic and charitable love.

The Chains of Metropolitan Culture

One of the leading Rousseau scholars of our time has written the following about Jean-Jacques Rousseau:

> A Swiss told the French that they did not know how to make love. What is even more astonishing, they believed him and took him as their master in the art of love. The Germans became the apprentices of the French, and in turn instructed the English. He, Rousseau that is, introduced them all to the *romantic*

taste—ideal and sincere—to take the place of their *gallantry*, which he treated as a school of vanity.[3]

The one work of Rousseau's most responsible for triggering a movement that we now refer to as the Romantic movement was *La Nouvelle Heloise.*

Rousseau's views on romantic love found in this novel are consistent with his political views. In stating that, "Man is born free; and everywhere he is in chains," he is not merely referring to chains of political oppression, but those of societal convention and opinion.[4] Man can only achieve true happiness (and true love) once these unnatural chains of civilization are lifted and he returns to a state of nature similar to that in which he was born. It is in *La Nouvelle Heloise* that he deals primarily with romantic love, a love chained (and made unsatisfactory) by societal convention.

Rather than attempting to repress what was considered to be potentially dangerous passions, Romanticism as a movement sought liberation and wholeness through the expression of romantic or erotic love. It was a movement which made such a love an *ideal.* This new ideal was intended to replace the notion that erotic love (*eros*) was not compatible with Christian love (*agape*). In writing *La Nouvelle Heloise*, Rousseau was writing about this seeming incompatibility within the context of the medieval love affair of Abelard and Heloise, an affair which ended tragically as a result of this perceived incompatibility.

The European reading public was extremely receptive to Romanticism. In fact, *La Nouvelle Heloise* was the best selling book of the eighteenth century. It was widely read throughout Europe. When first published in 1761, the initial demand for the book was so high among the public that it was rented out for the day and hour.[5] Twenty seven editions of the book were printed before 1800.[6]

Today, *La Nouvelle Heloise* is no longer read. In fact, it would not be a stretch to state that it is a "lost" book.[7] Perhaps due to its girth, or possibly its epistletory style, it does not appeal to the modern mass audience. We also may have lost the ability to understand or sympathize with the sentiment of love. This is unfortunate. Our general ignorance of this book has hampered us in our attempt to understand nineteenth century authors, like Dostoevsky, who did read it and who appear to be responding to its message.

La Nouvelle Heloise is a tragic novel, which focuses upon the unsuccessful/unfulfilled love affair between two lovers who live in a small Swiss village on the shores of Lake Leman (Lake Geneva). The natural setting of rural Switzerland seems ideal for the natural love of these two individuals. Unfortunately, the "chains" of civilization, as seen in the form of Julie's father and the class-based society of Switzerland of the time prohibits the marriage of Julie to her lowly tutor, St. Preux. Even though Julie eventually marries another man, St. Preux's passion for Julie never dies. At the end of the novel, we learn that Julie's passion for St. Preux also never dies.

This novel is tragic because society never allows the love of St. Preux and Julie to flourish. As a result, they both live unhappy lives. This denunciation of the civilized mores that kept these otherwise respectable and virtuous individuals from living complete lives was a message that resonated among the readership of Rousseau's day.

In concert with this message, Rousseau also took aim at yet a different source of discontent that struck at the very heart of the human sentiment of love—city life and its culture.

Paris and the Rise of Metropolitan Culture

For Rousseau, the evils of society are most clearly seen in the city—the most unnatural environment of man. Logically, Rousseau argues that it is here that individuals are in their most unhappy state. Speaking through a series of letters from St. Preux to Julie, Rousseau expertly describes the culture of Paris—a culture that could be dubbed metropolitanism.[8] He is quite systematic in his description, for in these letters he describes how Parisians think, feel and behave.[9]

Metropolitan Thinking

In letter XVII St. Preux describes for the rural Julie his images of the way that metropolitan Parisians think. For him, the key variable determining the city's mode of thought was its energy and motion. He writes that the city is a place of constant motion, a motion which precludes him from concentrating upon any single topic or reflecting upon it. He complains, ". . . I have no time to be moved by anything, nor to examine anything."[10] He continues this thought by writing, "The man of the world takes in everything and has time to reflect upon nothing."[11]

The non-reflective, fast-moving aspect of metropolitan life affects the manner in which Parisians interact with each other. St. Preux complains that he must lower his level of discourse due to the shallowness of urban thought. He writes that it is more important to be entertaining than learned in the city. In essence, humor replaces philosophy; social wit replaces wisdom and character.

St. Preux also found the Parisians to be faddish in the topics of their discussions. In letter XIV he writes that they, ". . . go out every evening to learn in their assemblies what they will think the next day."[12] In so doing, they sacrifice their freedom of thought to, ". . . a small number of men and women who think for all the others."[13]

Virtue, the product of reflection and effort, is replaced by social cleverness. Shame, which is felt upon virtue's failure, disappears. Ridicule takes its place. He writes that the Parisians,

> . . . are much more mocking than cutting, and come down less hard on vice than on the ridiculous. . . . What remains to be censured where virtue is no longer esteemed, and what could they vilify when they no longer think ill of anything? In Paris especially, where things are grasped only by their amusing side, anything that ought to provoke anger and indignation is always ill received if it is not put into song or epigram. Pretty women do not like to get

> cross, so nothing makes them cross; they like to laugh, and inasmuch as there is nothing to laugh about in crime, knaves are honest people like everyone else; but woe to the person who leaves himself open to ridicule, its caustic brand is indelible. . . .[14]

Predictably, the art form which dominates in this thoughtless, frivolous environment is comedy. St. Preux writes that the Parisian, ". . . seeks only wit and thoughts; he values amusement and not imitation, and does not ask to be persuaded provided he is entertained."[15] What is worse is that he is using this entertainment to inform his values. St. Preux writes that Parisians go to the theater, ". . . less to laugh at their follies than to study them, and becomes even more crazy than them by imitating them."[16] He concludes that in the city: ". . . the most sublime wisdom consists in living like fools."[17]

In their attempts to avoid ridicule, the behavior of Parisians is predictably conformist. He writes that they have one primary maxim: "One must do as the others do"[18] He is astounded that, ". . . everyone moves in time like the marches of a regiment in battle order: you would say that they are so many marionettes nailed to the same plank."[19]

Metropolitan Sentiment

Because of this shallow, faddish, frivolous, and conformist thinking, Parisians are unable to connect with each other in any meaningful way. St. Preux is deeply troubled by this, actually beginning his first letter from Paris by writing, "I enter with a secret horror into this vast desert of the world. This chaos presents me with nothing but horrible solitude, wherein reigns a dull silence."[20] He complains that illicit trysts comprise, ". . . all the tenderness and affection to be found in the liaisons of this country."[21] This results in a paradoxical loneliness in the midst of a crowd.

In essence, Parisians do not care for each other in a genuine sense; they are self-absorbed and vain. However, they mask their self-absorption in frequent discussions of sentiments. He writes that, "I can say I have never in my life heard so much talk about sentiment, nor so little understood what was being said about it."[22] The culture of the city has killed their sentiments. He concludes, "Thus they expend all their sentiment in wit, and so much of it is breathed out in talk that there remains none for practice."[23]

All of this, the death of deep thought and genuine sentiment, is the result of the turbulence and tumult of the city. The only element of Parisian society in which St. Preux finds sentiments is at the Opera. He discusses this in letter XXIII in which he writes,

> Each individual is not as free as you think to state his own opinion of this grave subject. Here anything is open to dispute except Music and the Opera. . . . French music is supported by a very stern inquisition, and the first thing that is whispered by way of instruction to all foreigners who come to this country is that all foreigners agree that there is nothing so beautiful in the rest of the world as the Paris Opera.[24]

He writes with incredulity, "But you could have no idea of the awful whines, the long howls with which the theater reverberates during the performance. The Actresses are seen almost in convulsions . . . their efforts cause as much suffering to those who are watching them as their singing does to those who are listening."[25]

It is at the Opera that Parisians invest their most prized sentiments. St. Preux concludes that these sentiments are ridiculous. In essence, the Parisian Opera functions as evidence for him that the Parisians had killed off the natural sentiments that should unite people one to the other. The result is a warped and perverse expression of non-human sentiments that is nothing short of ridiculous. These are the sentiments of an emotionally stunted people. He writes, ". . . what is bad entertains them more than what is good. They would rather scoff than applaud; the pleasure of criticizing compensates for the boredom of the spectacle, and they find it more agreeable to mock it when they are no longer there than to enjoy it while they are."[26]

Metropolitan Behavior

At first glance, metropolitan behavior appears to be quite civilized and pleasant. In letters XIV and XXI St. Preux reconsiders this and comes to the conclusion that metropolitan behavior is superficial, contrived, and unpleasant. Interestingly, he starts with the behavior of men and then moves to the behavior of women.

For St. Preux, the behavior of the metropolitan man is artificial, contrived, and false. Metropolitan men are focused exclusively upon externalities. They show, "false demonstrations of politeness, and the deceitful outward appearances which the ways of the world require."[27] He writes,

> One learns to plead artfully the cause of the lie, to unsettle with much philosophy all the principles of virtue, to color one's passions and prejudices with subtle sophisms, and to lend to error a certain stylish turn in keeping with the maxims of the day. It is not necessary to know the people's character, but only their interests, to make a fair guess about what they will say on every subject.[28]

He adds, "At each visit he must leave his soul at the door, if he has one; don one bearing the colors of the house. . . ."[29]

Ultimately, St. Preux found the behavior of Parisians to be so despicable because it was fundamentally hypocritical. He found that Parisians are constantly acting generous, but it is only an act. He writes, "Never did I hear so oft repeated: count on me when you need me; help yourself to my name, my purse, my house, my carriage. . . . Instead of that, this is perhaps of all the cities on earth the one where fortunes are most unequal."[30] He concludes this letter, "So far I have seen many masks; when shall I see men's faces."[31]

St. Preux was also discouraged with the behavior of Parisian women. For him, the city destroys the womanly virtues: in essence, women cease to be women. St. Preux writes, "It seems to have a deeper root in their manners, through the indiscreet and continual mixing of the two sexes, which leads each of them to adopt the air, language, and manners of the other."[32] He reiterates this toward the end of the letter, "The main objection to large cities is that there men become other than what they are, and society imparts to them, as it were, a being other than their own."[33] In other words, for Rousseau, men become women and women become men.

In spite of the gender-leveling quality of the city, women continue to superficially cling to womanly appearances. This is manifest in their focus upon fashion. He writes, "Fashion rules provincial ladies, but Parisian ladies rule fashion, and they can make it bend each to her own advantage."[34] The introduction of wealth induces the Parisian high-society women to guard their prerogatives through fashion. The high society women, because they are imitated by the country people, try to distinguish themselves by being scandalous. He writes, "They saw that an uncovered bust is a scandal to the public; they have considerably lowered their necklines."[35]

St. Preux found their behavior to be coarse. He writes, "Their bearing is devoid of affectation because they do not like constraint . . ."[36] He continues, "The tone is not the sweet and dainty one of our Vaudoises. It is a certain hard, acid, interrogative, imperious, mocking accent, and stronger than a man's. If in their tone there remains something of their sex's graces their intrepid and inquisitive manner of staring at people utterly eclipses it."[37]

Parisian women are as devoid of emotions as are the men, for such coarseness can not lead to love. He writes, ". . . whereas with modesty it can inspire a tender compassion that sometimes leads to love."[38] He continues,

> . . . what love can obtain where modesty is derided, and what charm can a life hold that is deprived at once of love and honesty? And so since the great scourge of all these dissipated people is boredom, the women are less concerned with being loved than being amused, to them being courted and served is more important than love, and provided a man is assiduous, it matters little that he be passionate. The very words love and lover are banished from the inner circles of both sexes. . . .[39]

Even within marriage love does not appear. He writes, "It seems that the whole order of natural sentiments is reversed here. The heart contracts no bonds, maidens are not allowed to have one. That right is reserved to married women, and excludes no one from their choice except their own husbands. It would be better for a mother to have twenty lovers than her daughter even one. Adultery causes no revulsion. . . ."[40] Marriage is nothing but the, ". . . consent of two free persons who agree to live together."[41]

Cosmopolitan Internationalism

From all this we can see that Rousseau is set upon blaming the city for the death of love, a condition which impoverishes human life. Interestingly, he is not content to stop there, for the death of love in the city actually results in the popularization of *cosmopolitanism* among urban dwellers. This is a paradoxical condition which requires some examination.

Today's cosmopolitanism is an ideal which celebrates worldliness.[42] It is an ethic which argues that parochial identities should be displaced by a global identity. In order to cultivate this global identity, traveling and maintaining links to other countries is seen as important. One should continuously seek knowledge of the practices of other countries and strive to maintain links with other nations. Ultimately, individuals should think of themselves as "citizens of the world."

It is important to note that the fundamental ideological quality of cosmopolitanism is equality. It is not an equality of citizens within a nation, but the equality of nations within the world. All nations are of equal worth; all cultures are of equal worth. Because no single culture can be looked at as being better than the other, national cultures take a back seat to a universal or *cosmopolitan* culture.

Rousseau felt that the cosmopolitan's professed love for the world was a gimmick designed to hide the fundamental flaw of cosmopolitanism. In *Emile*, Rousseau writes, "Distrust those cosmopolitans who go to great length in their books to discover duties they do not deign to fulfill around them. A philosopher loves the Tartars so as to be spared having to love his neighbors."[43] In the *Social Contract*, he amplifies this idea when he writes, "From this we can see what we should think of those so-called cosmopolitans who, justifying their love of their country through their love of the human race, boast of loving the whole world so as to have the right to love no one at all."[44]

In essence, Rousseau argues that one can not love people one does not know. The cosmopolitan insistence upon doing so, for Rousseau, illustrates little understanding of what love truly is. To use St. Preux's words about his observations of city people, "I can say I have never in my life heard so much talk about sentiment, nor so little understood what was being said about it."[45] The cosmopolitan's love of people in distant lands is not only a cover for not loving one's neighbor, but a cover for not being able to love in the first place.

The appeal to a global identity among urban cosmopolitans is also consistent with Rousseau's fundamental observation of the vanity of the urban dweller. Rousseau observes that virtually all people desire to be loved and admired. He argues that the source of admiration should be virtue, but that the city destroys virtue. In its place is social cleverness. One way to be clever is to be "worldly." Among cosmopolitans, to be worldly is to be clever because a worldly person displays hard-to-get knowledge. Any simpleton can learn what is happening to one's neighbors, but to know what is happening in a far-off country among a strange and exotic people is seen as the height of cleverness—and hence admired by cosmopolitans. This is precisely why Rousseau's great Russian devotee, Leo Tolstoy, began *War and Peace* (another great anti-cosmopolitan novel) with a society soiree at which the St. Petersburg cosmopolitan class discusses events in far-off France and Italy. Of course, most of this knowledge is trivial. Its pursuit and transmission only heightens the shallowness of the cosmopolitan for Rousseau.

Rousseau's reasoning which links the collapse of urban human sentiment with a cosmopolitan orientation is logically consistent. In point of fact, there are many other aspects of this link that can be examined. First and foremost is the simple fact that modern cities are the key players of global interdependence. With increasingly sophisticated levels of communication and transportation technology, the world has become a smaller and more interdependent place both economically and socially. With this comes the heightened realization of the importance of commercial and social cooperation. As nations become increasingly interdependent for wealth and well-being, the folly of interstate conflict becomes ever more apparent. Thus, being a city dweller simply puts one on the forefront of increasing levels of globalization with its consequent imperative that we are all inhabitants of the same "global village."

Because cities function as the international commercial and transportation centers in our modern world, cosmopolitans favor the city. This is often enhanced by the fact that these urban centers are often themselves the location in which cosmopolitan non-natives initially settle and live. In the nineteenth century it was common for French, Italian, Austrian, and Russian cosmopolitans to gather in the great European capitals and celebrate their worldliness (usually in French). Together they formed what was often called "high society."

There is, however, a less rational explanation for this link that is tied directly to metropolitan culture itself. The first simply involves the fact that metropolitan culture is a culture of the city, regardless of the surrounding "local" culture. This means that as cosmopolitans travel from city to city, they increasingly come to the realization that they truly are all, "citizens of the same world." Indeed, according to Rousseau (with only minor variations) the city will have the same effect upon individuals throughout the world. The city will always produce the same metropolitan culture. As St. Preux writes, "It is not Parisians I am studying, but the inhabitants of a large city, and for all I know what I see of it fits Rome and London just as well as Paris."[46]

Because cosmopolitanism is both a culture and an international political ideology, cosmopolitans can emphasize one or the other aspects. For instance, a cosmopolitan may choose to express his identity in terms of an adherence to worldly/universalistic political ideas. The ideas themselves may vary, ranging anywhere from Kantian universalism to Marxist socialism. The key common denominator is the rejection of nation as a primary ideological assumption. To be an ideological cosmopolitan, one must appear to embrace the negation of the nation as the fundamental political assumption of politics.

For those not politically oriented, there is another option. He may focus on certain behavioral, cultural, or linguistic traits that may be broadly defined as international or global culture. This cultural approach was quite popular in eighteenth and nineteenth century Russia among the Russian nobility who adopted European (mostly French) linguistic and cultural norms as their own.

This, of course, contributed to further consolidating the rigid and distinct political and economic class structure that was already in place before the advent of cosmopolitan culture there. Once again, the rejection of national cultural traits (language, dress, behavior) is seen as fundamental.

Nature's Cure

If the great metropolitan city of Paris represents the height of artificiality and the source of the soul's corruption, the remote mountains of Switzerland provide an ideal location for a cure for Rousseau. This is what we see in letter XXIII of *La Nouvelle Heloise.* In this letter we learn that St. Preux, having fled Vevey due to the inappropriate love he had for Julie, flees into the mountains of the Upper Valais. In his letter to Julie he writes that this has had a good effect on his soul.

He describes the landscape as rugged and wild. The diversity of nature in the mountains pleasantly strikes his eye, allowing him to contemplate, ". . . continual scenes that never ceased to elicit my admiration. . . ."[47] All in all, the mountains put him in a "peaceful state." He elaborates:

> Indeed, it is a general impression experienced by all men, although they do not all notice it, that high in the mountains where the air is pure and subtle, one breathes more freely, one feels lighter in the body, more serene in the mind; pleasures there are less intense, passions more moderate. Meditations there take on an indescribably grand and sublime character, in proportion with the objects that strike us, an indescribably tranquil delight that has nothing acrid or sensual about it. It seems that by rising above the habitation of men one leaves all base and earthly sentiments behind, and in proportion as one approaches ethereal spaces the soul contracts something of their inalterable beauty. . . . I wonder that baths of the salutary and beneficial air of the mountains have not become one of the principal remedies of medicine and morality.[48]

Nature is medicinal; among these mountains he finds a cure. He finds human relations among the mountain people to be simple and friendly. Being physically removed from commercial centers, they are free from the corruption of money. Living within small communities, they do not have the corrupting luxury of anonymity. They are also genuinely egalitarian. He writes, "Among themselves they behave in the same straightforward way; children of the age of reason are their fathers' equals, domestics eat at the same table with their masters; the same freedom reigns in homes as in the republic, and the family is the image of the State."[49]

The Idiot: Correcting Rousseau on Love

La Nouvelle Heloise is a novel devoted to the importance of natural and genuine love. Rousseau felt strongly about its importance. The fact that the city destroys these natural sentiments was, for him, quite serious. Dostoevsky was similarly appalled by cosmopolitanism. Just as Rousseau, he was particularly concerned about the death of love. It is in his second major novel, *The Idiot*, that Dostoevsky leveled his guns at this aspect of cosmopolitanism.

It is commonly believed that, *The Idiot*, is a novel about a Christ-like figure who attempts to live within modern society and fails. To many readers, this is a somewhat confusing notion. The novel's main protagonist, Lev Myshkin (the supposed Christ-like figure), hardly ever mentions God, he never speaks in parables (in fact he blathers on rather a lot), he conducts no miracles, and is not put to death at the end of the novel. In fact, he seems a naïve simpleton—an idiot.

This confusion disappears once we attempt to understand how Dostoevsky was attempting to address his readers who were steeped in Romantic literature. Through Myshkin, Dostoevsky was not attempting to re-create a Christ-like prototype, but was attempting to portray a man who expresses a "pure" form of Christian love—a love different from that idealized in *La Nouvelle Heloise*. In this sense, he was directly addressing how metropolitans *think, feel, and behave*.

The oft-overlooked link between *The Idiot* and *La Nouvelle Heloise* is astounding as we examine the many parallels between the two books. Both novels deal with romantic love as their primary themes. Both authors claimed to be attempting to portray a "beautiful soul."[50] Both novels denounce the falsity of human relations found in the city and high society. In fact, the main characters of both novels, Myshkin and St. Preux, seek a natural, healing wholeness in exactly the same area of the world—the Valais region of Switzerland.

The key difference between St. Preux and Myshkin is in the type of love they express. As seen above, St. Preux expresses a deeply romantic, and earthly, love for Julie. It is a passionate love akin to what we would call erotic love. Myshkin on the other hand is a character who feels and expresses charitable, Christian love. It is a "Christ-like" love insofar as it is never erotic. It is always selfless and sacrificial.

By re-creating a love-centered character like St. Preux, Dostoevsky is, in essence, correcting Rousseau on his notion of love. He agrees with Rousseau on the dangers of cosmopolitan culture. He also agrees with him on the naturalness of love and of its consequent redemptive value. What he wants to correct, however, is the purely romantic nature of Rousseau's understanding of love. Dostoevsky argues that the romantic approach to love (the deification of *eros*) is not the answer to the curse of urban civilization. Surprisingly, neither is the strict adherence to a purely charitable, Christ-like love. By starting and finishing with the "idiotic" condition of this Christ-like lover, Dostoevsky is condemning both the purely romantic as well as the purely charitable forms of romantic love.

The Story of *The Idiot*

The Idiot begins with the chance meeting of the two male characters on a late-November train speeding toward St. Petersburg: Lev Nikolayevich Myshkin and Parfyon Semyonovich Rogozhin. In the ensuing conversation, we learn that the twenty-six year old Myshkin is returning to Russia after an extended stay in Valais, Switzerland where he had gone for epilepsy treatment by a certain Dr. Schneider. Outwardly he is almost a comic image of the Swiss country gentleman with a pleasing, "thin and clean-cut" face in his hooded cape. (8:6)[51] In Russia, he shivers in his light Western garb, which is quite unsuitable for its winters.

Myshkin is "unpretentious and sincere." (8:7) Dostoevsky writes, "The readiness of the fair young man in the Swiss cloak to answer all his companion's inquiries was remarkable and betrayed no suspicion of the extreme impertinence of some of his [Rogozhin's] inappropriate and idle questions." (8:6) The overall effect of this behavior is fairly predictable: Myshkin likes others and others tend to reciprocate. Rogozhin approvingly declares that he is a, ". . . holy simpleton and God loves such as you." (8:14)

Rogozhin, on the other hand, is traveling back to St. Petersburg from Pskov, whence he had fled as a result of a fight with his father. The fight had been precipitated by the fact that he had expropriated 10,000 rubles from his father, bought a pair of diamond earrings with it, and had given these earrings to a woman with whom he had passionately fallen in love, Nastasya Filippovna Barashkova. Rogozhin fled after his father learned of this. He only returns to St. Petersburg once he learns that his father had died.

The contrast between these two figures could not be more clear: the meek, trusting Myshkin against the rude, combative Rogozhin. A clue as to what underlies this contrast can be found in the etymology of both characters' last names. Myshkin, derives from the Russian for "mouse" whereas Rogozhin's name is derived from the Russian word for "horn."[52] Thus, one is quiet, meek, and small while the other is wild and passionate.

Upon arriving in St. Petersburg, Rogozhin declares that he would like to see Myshkin again and show him a "good time" in the near future. Myshkin agrees, parts with him, and proceeds to the home of distant relatives whom he had never met—the Epanchins. Within this family, a family of high-standing and good reputation, we find three single, eligible young daughters. Myshkin's unpretentious, natural air disarms the normally aloof Epanchin family in much the same way as it did with Rogozhin on the train just hours before.

This first encounter with the Epanchin family goes well—and provides a prelude to the future romance between Myshkin and the youngest daughter—Aglaia. After finishing his visit with the Epanchins, Myshkin is found at his new accommodation—with the family of Gavrily Ardalyonovich (Ganya) Ivolgin, an employee of General Epanchin. Ganya also happens to be yet another suitor of Nastasya Filippovna.

It is here that Myshkin meets Nastaya Filippovna for the first time. She had come to the Ivolgins in order to humiliate Ganya, the man she had no intention of marrying. In the course of this visit, Rogozhin barges in, completely unaware that both she and Myshkin are also in the apartment. Rogozhin's intention is to intimidate Ganya into breaking with Nastasya Filippovna.

In the midst of this chaotic scene, Myshkin can see the explosive potential of the relationship between Nastasya Filippovna and Rogozhin. He concludes that Rogozhin will murder her if they marry. He believes that Rogozhin is driven by a morbid passion (*bol'noi strast'*), an unwholesome passion, or ungovernable desire, to possess her, but not to care for her. (8:28)

This scene ends with Nastasya Filippovna exiting the room with Rogozhin. Just before doing so, she states, "You know, I'm really not like this. . . ." (8:100) A similar scene follows that evening, at her birthday party, an occasion designed to determine her marital future. Ultimately, Ganya is rejected and humiliated. She is "purchased" by Rogozhin for 100,000 rubles.

In the midst of this chaos, Myshkin declares his love for Nastasya Filippovna. He states, "I . . . Nastasya Filippovna . . . I love you! I would die for you, Nastasya Filippovna! I will not let any one say a word about you. If we are poor, I'll work. . . ." (8:138) This unexpected outburst is then followed by the news that Myshkin is actually the heir to a sizable fortune (claiming this inheritance is what brought Myshkin to Russia from Switzerland to begin with).

By the end of part I, chapter 5, Myshkin has evinced his love for two quite different women—the dowry-laden Aglaia Epanchina and the high-society mistress Nastasya Filippovna. For the remainder of part I, Dostoevsky focuses upon the triangle centered upon Nastasya Filippovna (involving Myshkin and Rogozhin). He returns to the triangle centered upon Myshkin (involving Aglaia and Nastasya Filippovna) only in part II of the novel.

The action of part II takes place six months after the above-mentioned events. During this six month interval, Myshkin had traveled to Moscow, obtained his inheritance, and had returned to St. Petersburg as a properly dressed, society-oriented Prince Myshkin. Upon learning that the Epanchins were planning on spending the summer in Pavlovsk, he gives us a clue as to his motives by deciding to stay there as well.

Upon settling in Pavlovsk, he begins his pursuit of Aglaia Epanchina. From the very outset, however, Myshkin seems oddly out-of-place as a high-society gentleman or as a possible suitor to Aglaia. At one point (while still in Moscow) he writes a letter to Aglaia in which he states that he "needs her." However, when asked by Aglaia's mother, "Are you in love?" Myshkin states, "N-no. I . . . I wrote to her as to a sister; I signed myself as her brother." (8:264) Myshkin seems unclear about the type of love he feels toward Aglaia.

This lack of clarity is compounded by his feelings for Nastasya Filippovna. Upon his arrival in St. Petersburg (ostensibly to recommence the wooing of Aglaia), he seeks out Nastasya Filippovna! He finds Rogozhin's house and, although Rogozhin nearly kills Myshkin with a knife, they successfully recommence their friendship. Rogozhin understands that Myshkin does not represent a romantic rival. Myshkin has no desire to possess Nastasya; he loves her in a purely charitable way.

In essence, Myshkin is only able to love in a charitable way. In part II, he somewhat awkwardly explains to Rogozhin, "I do not love her with love (*lyubov'yu*) but with pity (*zhalost'yu*)." (8:173) For him, to love Nastasya Filippovna in a passionate manner was almost "unthinkable." (8:191) Myshkin elaborates upon this theme by stating that, "Compassion is the chief and perhaps only law of all human existence." (8:192) This, of course, contrasts with the "passionate" love that Rogozhin has for Nastasya. In fact, for Myshkin, Nastasya's face, ". . . even in the photograph, had roused in his heart [Myshkin's] a perfect agony of pity: the feeling of compassion and even of suffering over this woman never left his heart, and it had not even left it now. . . . He was certain, he was fully convinced for reasons of his own, that this woman was not psychologically stable (*pomeshannaya*)." (8:289)

The specific Russian words used here are important. In writing of the "agony of pity," Dostoevsky uses the words, *strandanie zhalosti*, otherwise translatable as the "suffering of pity." Indeed, Myshkin later explains that he can not even, "bear [to look at] Nastasya Filippovna's face." (8:484) He also states that he recognizes that she is seriously mentally unbalanced, but continues to love her with "all his entire soul." (8:484) In many ways, this is much more in keeping with the idea of compassion (at least in Russian), which is *sostradanie*—co-suffering. It seems quite plausible that in feeling a "compassionate" love for Nastasya, Myshkin is expressing a co-suffering attraction toward an individual who shares a desire to possess a complete form of love, one that is not purely erotic nor purely charitable.

To Aglaia, the young society damsel who understands wealth, power, and prestige, this sort of "compassionate" love for Nastasya Filippovna is no threat whatsoever. She compares Myshkin to a "poor knight" who symbolizes the platonic love of mediaeval chivalry as felt by, ". . . a pure and lofty knight." (8:207) She fails to recognize that he may very well not be able to feel love in any other way. She also does not take seriously the deep concerns that Myshkin feels about his attempt to integrate into St. Petersburg high society.

At the end of the day, Myshkin loves Aglaia, but in a purely charitable way. This is a form of love which does not flourish in the high-society world of the Epanchins. Their world is a world of power, prestige, money—and *eros*. Myshkin seems to sense this, and accepts that he will never be completely accepted in this world. This incompatibility can not lead to anything but a break with her, which occurs just after the party thrown in his honor by the Epanchins. Once this is accomplished, he renews his efforts to save Nastasya Filippovna from Rogozhin. In order to do this, he becomes engaged to her. On the very day of their marriage, Nastasya Filippovna flees Myshkin and returns to Rogozhin. As predicted by Myshkin at the very beginning of the novel, Rogozhin eventually kills her.

All of this pushes Myshkin into a state of despair. He returns to Switzerland in an even worse emotional and mental state than before. He retreats from reality, not able to understand any question asked of him, nor can he recognize any visitor. Dostoevsky concludes that, ". . . if Schneider himself had come from Switzerland to look at his former pupil and patient, and having remembered the condition in which Myshkin had sometimes been during the first year of his stay in Switzerland, he would have thrown up his hands in despair and would have said as he did then, 'An idiot.'" (8:507)

The Redemption of Christian Love

By having Myshkin begin and end in Switzerland, Dostoevsky is clearly addressing issues made famous by Rousseau in *La Nouvelle Heloise*. What is the nature of love? Can the artifices of society be overcome with the ideals of nature, to include that of romantic love? Through a vignette that he deliberately places in the Valais, Switzerland, Dostoevsky argues that it is not "nature" that cures, but a pure Christian love such as is found in children.

At the very beginning of *The Idiot*, in chapter 6, we find Myshkin recalling to the Epanchins the story of a young Swiss woman named Marie, who lives with her poor, old mother in a small house in a small Swiss village. At the beginning of the story, she is a weak, thin consumptive, but ever hardworking. One day, a traveling French businessmen seduces her and carries her off for about a week, after which time he leaves her. She returns to her village dirty, injured, bedraggled, crying, and miserable.

Her mother is furious that she had run off like this, thinking that it had dishonored her. Indeed, the village people publicly taunt Marie and shun her.[53] Although she is dying, Marie's mother never thinks of forgiving her daughter and kicks her out of the house, forcing her to sleep on a straw bed in a shed. She is given hardly enough food, going hungry most of the time.

In spite of all this, she gently nurses her ungrateful mother as she ails. She accepts such behavior as the price of her being a lowly creature. As her mother takes to her death bed, the old women of the village take it upon themselves to care for Marie's mother. They evict Marie from the house altogether, and cut her off financially. As no one in the village would give her a job, she roams the streets penniless. After her mother dies, Marie stands at her mother's coffin, "all in rags, crying" and yet the people continue to deride her. The pastor denounces her.

On top of the humiliation of public derision, Marie's health declines quickly. She begins to spit blood. Her clothes become so tattered that, ashamed to go into town, she retreats to the surrounding countryside where she begs a cowherd to take her on. Even he refuses her. She has no where else to go, so she watches after the cattle anyway.

Importantly, it is the children and Myshkin who begin the process of reversing the merciless treatment of Marie. Eventually the children stop ridiculing her in public and follow Myshkin's lead and begin to give her food and other provisions. Like Myshkin, they begin to love her. Eventually, as time goes by, Marie becomes the focus of the village children's every effort.

It then becomes clear that Marie is dying. The old women of the village follow the lead of the children and take turns in attending to her. When she does finally die, Myshkin recounts, "I assure you, that she died almost perfectly happy. Through them, she forgot her misery, as if she had obtained pardon from them, though she never ceased to consider herself a great sinner." (8:62-63)

The ultimate result of this is that the children gain a level of love for Myshkin as well. He becomes popular with them and reads them stories. For Myshkin, this is a labor of love, for he considers himself to be childlike. His doctor, Schneider, had said to him that he was a child and that he was only an adult, ". . . in size and face, but by development, spiritual and moral, and maybe even in intellect, [he was] . . . not an adult, and that [he would] . . . stay this way even until the age of sixty." (8:63) Myshkin himself admitted to preferring the company of children. He states, "Through children the soul is healed." (8:58)

For Myshkin, it is not a life in nature, or in Switzerland, or in romantic love that "cures" him. For him, it is the free and uncorrupted children who surround him while he is in Switzerland. Indeed, Myshkin believes that children are commonly misunderstood, that they are far more intelligent than we would believe. He states, ". . . they can actually teach us." (8:58) Indeed, the implication here is that the children can teach a "natural" love free from the corrupted love that they will learn later in life.

Two Types of Love

In creating two different characters, each representing a different type of love, Dostoevsky is attempting to illustrate the absurdity of a love which is either purely charitable or purely erotic. The dangers of the purely erotic love—the love idealized by the romantics—are clearly displayed by Rogozhin. His purely erotic love for Nastasya Filippovna is a possessive love, one in which he receives, and she must give. It is "morbid" insofar as it is an extreme version of erotic love. He must possess her, but so long as she has a free and individual will, his possession of her is always potentially threatened. The only way to *guarantee* his possession of her is to take away her will—by killing her. He does not kill her out of malice, but out of the most extreme desire to possess her. Indeed, even after he murders her, he places her on an alter and worships her.

The dilemma surrounding Myshkin's love for Aglaia and Nastasya is subtler—after all, how could anyone question the benevolence and purity of a Christ-like love which seeks to serve and sacrifice with no secondary motive? How could this possibly be denounced by a Christian writer such as was Dostoevsky? How could a love between Myshkin and Aglaia not blossom into happiness? Or with Nastasya?

Aglaia is the educated, society beauty. The fact that her name derives from the Greek word for splendor or beauty is important because erotic love often begins with an admiration of the object's beauty. Aglaia's beauty, however, is not only skin deep. She is rich, prestigious, and from a powerful family. She is the logical target for any man's possessive longings. As the symbol of "pure" charitable love, Myshkin does not feel such an erotic love for her. He loves her, but in the same way that a brother loves a sister. This makes him a highly inappropriate choice for a romantic relationship with Aglaia.

To take this brotherly love one more step—Myshkin loves Aglaia like a rich, beautiful, smart sister who has everything in life. He loves her but does not "pity" her. This is what contrasts his love for Aglaia with that of Nastasya Filippovna, who is also a beautiful woman, but with a disreputable past. We learn that she was originally from a good family that had fallen upon hard times. Her father had died from grief after having learned that his wife had tragically died in a home fire while he was away on business. A neighbor named Totsky agreed to raise the two surviving children immediately after this calamity. Shortly thereafter, one of the two children died, leaving the child Nastasya Filippovna as the sole survivor of her immediate family. Eventually Totsky, a Westernized man of the world, seduced her and made her his kept mistress.

As virtually any Russian-language reader of this novel would immediately know, the name Nastasya is the shortened form for the Russian name, Anastasia. This name originally comes from the Greek word *anastasios* meaning "resurrection." Her rarely mentioned last name, Barashkova, comes from the Russian word *barashek,* meaning "lamb." Her combined name conveys perhaps the most Christian of all symbols, that of a "resurrected lamb." She is the lamb to be sacrificed at the alter of Rogozhin's (and Totsky's) morbid possessive, erotic love.

All of this makes Nastasya a pitiful creature, and therefore more "lovable" in a Christian sense. She had lost the family that loved her and found no one else that could replace it. Because of her beauty, all she found were men motivated by lust. When Myshkin declares his love (a purely charitable love) she seems to lose her bearings on reality. Dostoevsky writes, "It was asserted afterwards that it was at this moment Nastasya Filippovna went mad." (8:140)

Dostoevsky uses the word *pomeshannaya* to describe Nastasya Filippovna's new condition. This is usually translated as mad or crazy or insane. The root of this word is linked to the Russian word for "mixer"—*meshalka.* In essence, she lost her ability to reason because she is "mixed up." How? She falls in love with Myshkin because of his goodness. In loving him, however, she does not want to sully his honor by associating with him.[54] Myshkin himself understands this. At one point he explains to Aglaia that Nastasya Filippovna has an, ". . . inner craving to do something shameful, so as to say to herself at once, 'There, you've once again done a shameful thing, you a low creature!' . . . Do you know that in that continual consciousness of shame for her there is perhaps a sort of awful, unnatural enjoyment, as if it were a revenge of some sort upon someone." (8:361) It is enjoyable to her because it allows her to escape the trap of potentially hurting someone she loves by precluding the possibility of love in the first place.

Myshkin also understands that a "healthy" love contains within it a seemingly contradictory element. He admits this when he says, in one often-overlooked passage, in which Myshkin himself admits to suffering from "double thoughts." In a conversation with Keller, one of the most grotesque figures of the novel, Myshkin explains to him his belief that people can have both altruistic and selfish thoughts at the same time. Myshkin states that, "The two thoughts come together; that often happens. With me it is constant. By the way, I think that it's not a good thing; and do you know, Keller, I reproach myself most of all for it . . . it is awfully difficult to struggle against these double thoughts; I have tried." (8: 258)

This is the key. Dostoevsky adheres to Christian teachings on the nature of love which holds that the highest from of romantic love is a Christian charitable love, *agape*, which is often informed by *eros*.[55] For Christians, such as Dostoevsky, *eros* is a form of love which needs to be cultivated, disciplined, and purified if it can ever lead to the higher form of self-less, sacrificing love of *agape* within the context of a romantic relationship. Romanticism idealizes *eros*—makes it divine; justifying it as "natural" and "beautiful." Christianity tames it, channels it, sublimates it and amalgamates it into *agape*.

Dostoevsky's *The Idiot* tells us that the failure to understand love properly is tragic. Rousseau's erotic love, as found in *La Nouvelle Heloise*, ends with Rogozhin's sad fate. A purely charitable love, as found in Myshkin's story, meets with a similarly sad fate. For Dostoevsky, the tragedy of the Romantic era was the failure to accept that *eros* and *agape* must work together. If *eros* and *agape* are not working together, one can not avoid the fate of either Myshkin or Rogozhin.

From *The Idiot* to *The Demons*

In *The Idiot*, Dostoevsky announces that Rousseau did not understand the nature of true love. In *The Demons* he argues that Rousseau did not understand the magnitude of the cosmopolitan problem. Here, Dostoevsky presents us with a political and psychological critique of cosmopolitanism. Cosmopolitanism not only results in the death of love, but in *The Demons* we see that it results in political despotism and nihilism.

Although he continues to agree with Rousseau that cosmopolitanism kills reflective thinking, stifles the sentiments, and creates artificiality in human relations, we have several clear indicators that Dostoevsky's intent in *The Demons* is, once again, to correct the message of *La Nouvelle Heloise*. Dostoevsky actually begins his conceptualization of *The Demons* by having Karuzov (aka. Lebyadkin) live in Julie's hometown of Vevey, Switzerland before the start of the action of the book. (11:55) Although this character changes significantly in the final work, Dostoevsky has the romantic plot line begin in Switzerland in the notional town of Vernay-Montreaux.[56] Clearly, this is meant to signal a parallel to the genuine town of Vevey, which—being linked to the neighboring town of Montreaux—is often referred to as Vevey-Montreaux. Nineteenth century readers would have recognized this parallel immediately. In fact, they would have appreciated the slight alteration in the name of the town. By slightly changing the name of this Swiss town, Dostoevsky is alluding to the "goodness" of this place. The word *vernyj* in Russian is usually translated as "correct" or "right." He is thus adding a bit here. It is not only the perfect place for Rousseau's sentiment of love, but it is "correct" and a "right" place.

Dostoevsky's nineteenth century readers would have also recognized, and enjoyed, the contrast between Julie/St. Preux and the two middle-aged protagonists of *The Demons* of Stepan Trofimovich/Varvara Petrovna. Both couples exchange letters frequently and keep them for posterity. Stepan Trofimovich, like St. Preux, is also a hired tutor who teaches in the house of Varvara Petrovna. Most importantly, Stepan Trofimovich and Varvara Petrovna bear all of the traits of St. Preux's Parisians—they are shallow, vain and lacking in content. As cosmopolitans, they lack the capacity to form and maintain meaningful relationships. Significantly, both mimic the culture of Paris linguistically and socially. In fact, Stepan Trofimovich, like most of Russia's nineteenth century elite, feels more comfortable speaking French than Russian.

Although the word "cosmopolitan" never made its way into *The Demons*, Dostoevsky meant for murdered former terrorist, Shatov, to represent its opposite. In describing this character, he wrote in his notebooks for the novel, "Shaposhnikov [aka. Shatov]—a native type. . . .This is not a matter of conviction: this is the final results of Peter the Great's reforms. He decided that his Russians must become Europeans by decree, and 150 years later he got them, under the conditions in which they have become alienated from their own people and not attached to any others. This is because all the others are nations, whereas we deny nationality on principle, wanting to be pan-Europeans, although there just is not such a thing as a pan-European." (11:66)

Dostoevsky does, however, mention the term "cosmopolitan" twice in the notebooks for *The Demons*. Dostoevsky has Shatov state, "We can not have either family, or familial virtues, because a family can not be cosmopolitan [*kosmopoliticheskoe*] and is destroyed the very moment it is severed from its native land. And we have cursed our native land; many are merely indifferent toward it." (11:94)[57] Later in the notebooks, he writes, "A cosmopolitan cannot be an honest man (this is the conviction of Shaposhnikov [aka. Shatov])." (11:119)

Why did Dostoevsky not use the term "cosmopolitan" in the novel itself? It seems likely that the term then, as today, had a very positive connotation. He may very well have feared that by associating this term with terrorist activities, he would have created such consonant dissonance so as to preclude understanding of his intended message.

Although he does not mention the term "cosmopolitanism," he does refer to Rousseau by name in *The Demons*. In the controversial chapter "At Tikhon's" we read the following sentence in Stavrogin's confession: "Giving myself with extraordinary immoderation, until the age of sixteen, to the vice confessed by Jean-Jacques Rousseau, I stopped it the moment I decided I wanted to, in my seventeenth year." (11:14) Dostoevsky obviously felt that he did not need to explain exactly what this vice was.[58] He assumed that his reader would simply know this, because any literate person of the 1870's had read Rousseau's *Confessions*.[59]

Much like Rousseau, Dostoevsky felt that cosmopolitanism was extremely destructive. He agreed with Rousseau that cosmopolitanism destroys ideals—and consequently both love and meaning. As we shall shortly see, Dostoevsky elaborates upon this theme in *The Demons*. He argues that cosmopolitanism also has certain political and psychological effects that must be examined. Through this examination, we can observe how cosmopolitanism, paradoxically, ends in political despotism and terrorism. Let us now, in the following chapter, examine how he arrives at this conclusion.

Notes

1. Richardson's *Clarissa*, another epistolary work, was also famous at the time. Having a French education, it seems likely *La Nouvelle Heloise*, not *Clarissa*, was more influential on him.

2. Rousseau's influence upon Dostoevsky's great contemporary, Leo Tolstoy, is well-known and well-documented. Strangely, Rousseau's influence upon Dostoevsky receives less attention. See Robin Feuer Miller, *Imitations of Rousseau in* The Possessed, Dostoevsky Studies 5 (1984): 77-90. Found at: http://www.utoronto.ca/tsq/DS/05/077.shtml (17 October 2008).

3. Allan Bloom, *Love and Friendship* (New York: Simon & Schuster, 1993): 39.

4. Jean-Jacques Rousseau, *The Social Contract and Discourses* (London: J. M. Dent/Everyman, 1993) : 181.

5. Robert Darnton, *The Great Cat Massacre and Other Episodes in French Cultural History* (New York: Basic Books, 1984): 242.

6. Robert Darnton, *The Great Cat Massacre and Other Episodes in French Cultural History*, 242.

7. *La Nouvelle Heloise* is not even mentioned by Allan Bloom in his chapter on Rousseau found in the seminal Strauss/Cropsey reader on political philosophy. See Allan Bloom, "Jean-Jacques Rousseau," in Leo Strauss and Joseph Cropsey, *History of Political Philosophy, 3rd Edition* (Chicago: University of Chicago Press, 1987): 559 – 580. Dr. Mark Kremer is single-handedly responsible for resurrecting an awareness of this "lost" book in the English-speaking world.

8. I am deeply indebted to Dr. Mark Kremer for comments and suggestions relating to Rousseau. I take, however, a somewhat different approach to this novel than he does.

9. I am analyzing cosmopolitanism in a manner similar to the way in which Tocqueville approached an understanding of American culture in book II of *Democracy in America*. I have changed the order for ease of description. See Alexis de Tocqueville, *Democracy in America*, trans. Harvey Mansfield and Delba Winthrop (Chicago: University of Chicago Press, 2002).

10. Jean-Jacques Rousseau, *Julie or the New Heloise: Letters of Two Lovers Who Live in a Small Town at the Foot of the Alps*, trans. Philip Steward and Jean Vache (London: University Press of New England, 1997): 201.

11. Jean-Jacques Rousseau, *Julie or the New Heloise*, 202.

12. Jean-Jacques Rousseau, *Julie or the New Heloise*, 192.

13. Jean-Jacques Rousseau, *Julie or the New Heloise*, 192.

14. Jean-Jacques Rousseau, *Julie or the New Heloise*, 203.

15. Jean-Jacques Rousseau, *Julie or the New Heloise*, 207.

16. Jean-Jacques Rousseau, *Julie or the New Heloise*, 207.

17. Jean-Jacques Rousseau, *Julie or the New Heloise,* 209.
18. Jean-Jacques Rousseau, *Julie or the New Heloise,* 205.
19. Jean-Jacques Rousseau, *Julie or the New Heloise,* 205.
20. Jean-Jacques Rousseau, *Julie or the New Heloise,* 190.
21. Jean-Jacques Rousseau, *Julie or the New Heloise,* 204.
22. Jean-Jacques Rousseau, *Julie or the New Heloise,* 205.
23. Jean-Jacques Rousseau, *Julie or the New Heloise,* 205.
24. Jean-Jacques Rousseau, *Julie or the New Heloise,* 230.
25. Jean-Jacques Rousseau, *Julie or the New Heloise,* 233.
26. Jean-Jacques Rousseau, *Julie or the New Heloise,* 236.
27. Jean-Jacques Rousseau, *Julie or the New Heloise,* 190.
28. Jean-Jacques Rousseau, *Julie or the New Heloise,* 191.
29. Jean-Jacques Rousseau, *Julie or the New Heloise,* 192.
30. Jean-Jacques Rousseau, *Julie or the New Heloise,* 191.
31. Jean-Jacques Rousseau, *Julie or the New Heloise,* 194.
32. Jean-Jacques Rousseau, *Julie or the New Heloise,* 220.
33. Jean-Jacques Rousseau, *Julie or the New Heloise,* 223.
34. Jean-Jacques Rousseau, *Julie or the New Heloise,* 218.
35. Jean-Jacques Rousseau, *Julie or the New Heloise,* 219.
36. Jean-Jacques Rousseau, *Julie or the New Heloise,* 217.
37. Jean-Jacques Rousseau, *Julie or the New Heloise,* 220.
38. Jean-Jacques Rousseau, *Julie or the New Heloise,* 220.
39. Jean-Jacques Rousseau, *Julie or the New Heloise,* 221.
40. Jean-Jacques Rousseau, *Julie or the New Heloise,* 222.
41. Jean-Jacques Rousseau, *Julie or the New Heloise,* 222.
42. Kwame Anthony Appiah reminds us that cosmopolitanism finds its roots in ancient Greece among the Cynics who saw themselves as "citizens of the cosmos." This signaled a ". . . rejection of the conventional view that every civilized person belonged to a community among communities." See Kwame Anthony Appiah, *Cosmopolitanism: Ethics in a World of Strangers* (New York: Norton, 2006): xiv.
43. Jean-Jacques Rousseau, *Emile or On Education*, trans. Allan Bloom (New York: Basic Books, 1979): 39.
44. Jean-Jacques Rousseau, *The Social Contract and The Discourses* (London: Everyman's Library, 1993): 175.
45. Jean-Jacques Rousseau, *Julie or the New Heloise,* 205.
46. Jean-Jacques Rousseau, *Julie or the New Heloise,* 199.
47. Jean-Jacques Rousseau, *Julie or the New Heloise,* 63.
48. Jean-Jacques Rousseau, *Julie or the New Heloise,* 64.
49. Jean-Jacques Rousseau, *Julie or the New Heloise,* 66.
50. Jean-Jacques Rousseau, *Julie or the New Heloise, 8.* See also Murray Krieger, "Dostoevsky's 'Idiot': The Curse of Saintliness," in *Dostoevsky: A Collection of Critical Essays*, ed. Rene Wellek (Englewood Cliffs, N.J.: Prentice-Hall, 1962): 39.
51. F. M. Dostoevsky, *Polnoe Sobranie Sochinenii i Pisem*, 30 vols. (Leningrad: Nauka, 1972-1990). All parenthetical references within the text are by volume and page number to this Academy edition. Translations are my own, although I was considerably aided in this by Constance Garnett's translation.
52. It should also be noted that Lev Nikolayevich is the name and patronymic of Leo Tolstoy, a Rousseauean model for Myshkin. See Donna Orwin, "The Return to Nature: Tolstoyan Echoes in *The Idiot*," *Russian Review* 58 (January 1999): 87.

53. It is interesting to note that these mountain people do not at all resemble the mountain people of Rousseau's *La Nouvelle Heloise*.

54. In the end, her selfless agape for Myshkin compels her to return to Rogozhin and certain death. In essence, her desire to not dishonor Myshkin by marrying him, compelled her to sacrifice herself to save him.

55. There is probably no better book on this than C. S. Lewis, *The Four Loves* (New York: Harcourt, 1988).

56. In nineteenth century Russian literature it was common practice to supply notional names for small towns.

57. In reality, the preparatory notebooks for *The Demons* are only partially useful. Not only did Dostoevsky never intend for these to be read, but the utility of any single note is questionable due to the dramatic changes that we see within the notebooks themselves. Wasiolek cautions us in the regard when he writes in his English-language translation of these notebooks, ". . . in December he [Dostoevsky] complained to Strakhov that he had revised the novel at least ten times, and in January 1871, to his niece, that he had revised it at least twenty times. . . . Nor is he sure what he is writing. . . ." See Fyodor Dostoevsky, *The Notebooks for* The Possessed, ed., Edward Wasiolek, trans., Victor Terras (Chicago: University of Chicago Press, 1968): 5.

58. The vice was masturbation.

59. While this worked well for readers of his day, it is a handicap today as this grounding in these "classic" works is largely absent.

Chapter 3
Cosmopolitan Politics

Near the beginning of *The Demons*, Dostoevsky has the novel's narrator observe a seemingly innocuous event. He recollects that the novel's main character, Stepan Trofimovich Verkhovensky, ". . . would take Tocqueville with him to the garden, but with Paul de Kock hidden in his side pocket." (10:19) Rather than reading the weightier Tocqueville, Stepan Trofimovich amuses himself with a light novel. Why is Tocqueville mentioned here? What is the significance of Stepan Trofimovich's neglect of Tocqueville?

Dostoevsky does not mention Tocqueville in a fit of absent-mindedness. In point of fact, hidden within this reference, is a clue as to what Dostoevsky intends to convey with regard to the *political* message of *The Demons*. By ignoring Tocqueville, the cosmopolitan Stepan Trofimovich is committing a tragic error. His neglect of Tocqueville results in his failure to understand the ramifications of the ideology he personifies—cosmopolitanism.

For Dostoevsky, cosmopolitanism has a political as well as a cultural face. Stepan Trofimovich personifies both of them.[1] On the cultural level, he rejects Russia's cultural roots—its traditions, customs, language, and religion. He adheres to cosmopolitan cultural practices, described so nicely by Jean-Jacques Rousseau in *La Nouvelle Heloise*.[2] On the political level, Stepan Trofimovich holds allegiance to only one political principle—the principle that lies at the very heart of cosmopolitan politics—its spirit of national and international equality.

In adhering to the political and cultural aspects of cosmopolitanism simultaneously, a singularly unique amalgamation is created—rootless egalitarianism. While Dostoevsky portrays this in a most absurd manner through the character of Stepan Trofimovich, it is its product with which he is primarily concerned—the despotic and terroristic Pyotr Stepanovich Verkhovensky. In other words, for Dostoevsky, cosmopolitan politics and culture, which by definition is rootless egalitarianism, ends in despotic terrorism.

Dostoevsky is primarily a writer who focuses upon those things psychological. It is logical, therefore, that he focuses upon the cultural aspects of cosmopolitanism more than upon the political aspects. Indeed, *The Demons* is replete with descriptions of Stepan Trofimovich's cultural cosmopolitanism. Alexis de Tocqueville, of course, is a purely political writer. The primary focus of his book, *Democracy in America*, is upon the primacy of the political concept of equality in America and its effects upon American institutions, beliefs, and behavior. Although he never mentions the word "cosmopolitanism," he quite clearly argues that rootless egalitarianism represents the fatal flaw of democracy. In other words, he argues that if American democracy should ever lose its roots (for Tocqueville found primarily in religion), a democratic despotism will result.

The fundamental political message of both of these writers is thus strikingly similar. Because Dostoevsky emphasizes the cultural aspects of cosmopolitanism, while Tocqueville emphasizes its political aspects, we gain a greater insight into cosmopolitanism and its effects by reading and analyzing both.

The Vain Cosmopolitan

Stepan Trofimovich, the central character of *The Demons*, is a cosmopolitan *par excellence*. He is an empirical, rational, atheist who embraces political equality and is international in orientation and loyalty. Importantly, however, he is more committed to the form of these ideas rather than to their substance. In essence, his cosmopolitanism is driven by *vanity*, and as a vain cosmopolitan, Stepan Trofimovich is less concerned with the content of his ideological ideas than with how he appears espousing these ideas. It is significant that Dostoevsky feels compelled to mention in the initial description of Stepan Trofimovich that his identity as a man of the world is, ". . . gratifying to his vanity." (10:7) He is a self-absorbed intellectual, who is obsessed with his own empty ideas and how they appear to others.

Because vanity is at the root of all things he does, any attack upon Stepan Trofimovich's self-determined importance is devastating. We first see this happen at the very beginning of the novel as Varvara Petrovna and Stepan Trofimovich travel together to St. Petersburg in order for him to make an "appearance" and be "appreciated" among the intelligentsia there. (10:23) After publicly proclaiming his beliefs at a meeting there, "He was hissed so mercilessly that he burst into tears right there, publicly, before he even got off the platform." (10:23) Pathetically, Varvara Petrovna brought him home, ". . . more dead than alive." (10:23)

Varvara Petrovna subsequently sends him to the West where he could be properly appreciated. Stepan Trofimovich himself believes that such a move will "resurrect" him. (10:24) We subsequently learn that his empty ideas are not appreciated there either. He retreats back to Russia prematurely, incorrectly claiming that his early return is due to the heartache he experienced there because the area reminded him of his son.

This vanity-driven attraction to cosmopolitanism indicates a shallow commitment to its underlying ideas, a shallowness that precludes deeper reflection upon its potentially disastrous ideological ramifications. On the individual level, his lack of reflection leads to the neglect of his son, the unconsummated character of his mutually unsatisfying relationship with Varvara Petrovna, and a whole host of other absurd situations in which he finds himself throughout the novel. On the ideological level, his ideas end in despotism.

It is also significant that *The Demons* opens with a presentation of Stepan Trofimovich as a "persecuted" man who believes that he was banished to the provinces for his progressive political beliefs. (10:7)[3] Unlike many of his parochial fellow countrymen, he is a well-traveled, educated, and urbane polyglot. He considers himself to be progressive, liberal, and open-minded, not constrained by local traditions, customs and laws. He does not adhere to any particular religious belief and rejects dogmas or formulations of absolute truth. Consequently, he relies upon his own reason to be the arbiter of right and wrong. As with other cosmopolitans, this focus upon self-reliance results in an excessive form of individualism.

As a cosmopolitan, Stepan Trofimovich not only rejects traditions, customs, and laws, but traditional behavioral practices found in Russia at that time. To a nineteenth century Russian reader, the absurdity of his insecurities and neuroses is exacerbated by his failure to abide by the traditional gender and generational roles of the Russian man of that period. Throughout the novel he remains emotionally and financially dependent upon the women in the novel and consistently seeks consolation from his school-age pupils when insulted.

Throughout the novel, there is only one admiring audience for Stepan Trofimovich's ideas—Varvara Petrovna. This explains his attraction to her. When, at one point in the novel, it appears that another intellectual, the acclaimed writer Karamazinov, might displace him in her eyes as the local intellectual, he reacts strongly. He claims that she is acting "despotically." For him, her focus upon Karamazinov was, ". . . the most offensive and cruel despotism that can possibly exist in the world." (10:73) It is offensive and cruel because it threatens the one thing he lives for—his vain need for the approval of others. Varvara Petrovna is in an enormously powerful position as the sole gratifier of his vanity. So long as she fulfills this role, Stepan Trofimovich is content. By arbitrarily taking this away, she becomes a "despot."

Stepan Trofimovich's role in creating this despot is critical. He cares for Varvara Petrovna only insofar as she provides for him the ability to love himself by gratifying his vanity. Varvara Petrovna alone seems to understand this when she states that their twenty-year friendship was nothing more than, ". . . reciprocal self-love." (10:263) She elaborates by saying, "Your every letter to me was written not for me but for posterity." (10:263)

Stepan Trofimovich's relations with other women in this novel also illustrate his desire to obtain the sort of maternal and unconditional love that is often seen between a mother and son. Stepan neither flatters nor pursues women. He never appears to desire a sensuous being or a sexual relationship. He is simply a boy seeking maternal love. This appears to be the case with his two earlier marriages.

His first marriage, to a "flighty" and attractive girl from "our" province lasted effectively only a couple of years, after which time he was separated from her for an additional three years. This marriage was doomed as a result of the fact that Stepan Trofimovich could not support her materially. The narrator also writes that the marriage ended for somewhat "delicate" reasons as well. (10:11) In other words, Stepan Trofimovich could not fulfill her romantic needs. She left him a five-year-old son upon her death (Pyotr Stepanovich).

His second marriage, which lasted less than a year, was to a, ". . . quiet little German woman from Berlin." (10:11) Her premature death brought an end to this marriage. Although nothing else is said about this marriage, the implication of her early death is that Stepan failed to take care of her as well.

The fact that he wants more of a mother figure than a wife is indicated by the fact that he is willing to go along with Varvara Petrovna's plan to marry him off to Darya Pavlovna (Dasha), a woman who committed a sexual indiscretion in Switzerland. This willingness is buttressed with his philosophical support of a "woman's freedom." He explains that, ". . . Christianity has never understood woman—as has been so splendidly revealed by George Sand in one of her brilliant novels." (10:33) In other words, he unequivocally supports the notion of absolute equality, even if it means a woman's sexual freedom within marriage.

Stepan Trofimovich might be somewhat delusional here. It could very well be that it is his vanity that is driving his beliefs about the role of women in his life. In essence, a woman who is not loyal in marriage is not so bad so long as she is motherly in her attentions toward him. Of course, this is the root of his completely asexual relationship with Varvara Petrovna.

Interestingly, Stepan Trofimovich does feel shame about being forced into a marriage to Dasha. He is not in the least concerned about her "sins," nor for the fact that he was being forced to marry her. His concern revolves around the fact that he is being forced into a marriage in which he would not be the sole actor of his universe. He explains, "Oh, my friend, marriage is the moral death of any proud soul, of any independence. Married life will corrupt me and rob me of my energy, my courage in serving the cause. There will be children, perhaps not even mine, that is, certainly not mine—the wise are not afraid to look truth straight in the face. . . ." (10:100) Once again, it is his vanity that clouds what is clearly an absurd situation.

The absurdity of this man-child, and his bizarre relations with women, never ends. Just as a child finds the idea of life without a mother to be intolerable, Stepan Trofimovich cannot be without a mother figure in his life at any time in the book. Even after he leaves the protective cocoon provided by Varvara Petrovna on his last "quest," he meets up with, and fervently latches onto Sofya Matveevna Ulitin. He is, due to this psychological need to have someone feed his vanity, totally dependent upon maternal women out of a desire to receive motherly recognition, admiration, and appreciation.

The Cosmopolitan Scholar

Vanity is the paradoxical combination of self-conceit, desire for admiration, as well as a description of an object lacking in value. Stepan Trofimovich, in this sense, exhibits all of these characteristics. As a vain cosmopolitan he feels that he will be admired based upon his cosmopolitan appearances and practices. Unfortunately, his cosmopolitan ideas are lacking in meaning and significance.

His self-conceit and desire for admiration are manifest in his tendency to lecture, rather than discuss his ideological views. To put it another way, he professes his views. It is therefore no surprise that Praskovya Ivanovna simply refers to him as "professor." (10:54) This long-winded style makes him a tiresome companion. In one characteristic outburst, Varvara says, "Abbreviate if you can, Stepan Trofimovich." (10:48)

Stepan Trofimovich's vanity is not only a sign of self-conceit and a desire for admiration, but also an indicator of the low quality of his ideas. As mentioned above, he lacks the ability to reflect upon his ideas. This seems to be caused first and foremost by his restlessness. In his initial description of Stepan Trofimovich, the narrator writes that Stepan's name, ". . . was uttered by many hurrying people of that day almost on par with the names of Chaadaev, Belinksy, Granovsky, and Herzen. . . ." (10:8) Individuals who "hurry" often find it impossible to reflect. To make this even clearer, the narrator writes, "He [Stepan] could not endure solitude and constantly longed for someone to entertain him at once." (10:52)

Without reflection or thought, it is no wonder that his scholarly work remained irrelevant, unknown, and opaque. The narrator recalls a poem written by Stepan Trofimovich, which had once been seized in Moscow by the authorities for being politically subversive. Somewhat humorously the narrator recalls that six years previous to this, the poem had been circulated in the West among two enthusiasts and one student. (10:9) Because Stepan Trofimovich takes so much pride in his "persecuted" status; it seems natural that he would be anxious to allow the narrator to read it. Indeed, he received a hand-written copy (by Stepan Trofimovich himself), with his inscription, and bound in magnificent red morocco. (10:9) The narrator informs us that he found it difficult to give the plot, ". . . because to tell the truth I did not understand anything within it." (10:9)

The fact that Stepan Trofimovich is lazy might also contribute to the irrelevance of his work. The narrator writes that he, at one point, published an article in a monthly "progressive" journal. He writes, ". . . the beginning of a most profound study—having to do, apparently, with the reasons for the remarkable moral nobility of some knights in some epoch, or something of the sort." (10:9) Unfortunately, the sequel was never published because, "the author himself was too lazy to finish the study." (10:9)

Like many an academic that has little of significance to say, Stepan Trofimovich chose to specialize in esoteric topics. It is recalled in the novel, that at the end of the 1840's, upon returning to Russia, he, ". . . managed to defend a brilliant thesis on the emerged civil and Hanseatic importance of the German town of Hanau, in the period between 1413 and 1428, together with the peculiar and vague reasons why that importance never took place." (10:8) While Dostoevsky was clearly negatively alluding to Russian Westernizer/Academic T. N. Granovsky, he was also belittling any academic that conducts research of such limited scope, interest, and significance.

Cosmopolitan Egalitarianism

Up to this point we have referred to Stepan Trofimovich as a man who embraces a cosmopolitan outlook and culture. Interestingly, we have few clues about his political beliefs other than the fact that he believes in "equality" and is therefore opposed to Tsarist autocracy. Because of this, Stepan Trofimovich considers himself to be a "reproach incarnate" to his fatherland. (10:11)

Although never stated directly, Stepan Trofimovich considers himself to be a member of the Russian *intelligentsiya*. The irony of this is usually lost on the Western reader. Although the nineteenth century Russian word *intelligentsiya* gave birth to the modern English language concept of "intelligentsia," the two concepts are slightly different. The emphasis in the English-speaking world is primarily upon the fact that the intelligentsia is a group that aspires to intellectual and cultural activity. Such bohemians can be found in such artistic places as Soho and Hampstead. They tend to be political activists only as an afterthought.

The Russian *intelligentsiya* is somewhat distinct from this insofar as political activism is a primary activity. In essence, the Russian *intelligentsiya* was a social category based upon a certain consciousness and a certain set of moral, ethical, philosophical, social and political values.[4] A Russian *intelligent* was fundamentally a believer in equality and an activist in pursuit thereof.[5] This made them, above all else, enemies of Tsarist autocracy. To put it differently, a Russian *intelligent* was a man of public virtue. This is precisely why the narrator in *The Demons* writes that Stepan Trofimovich bases his identity upon his "civic role" and that he, ". . . loved this role to the point of passion—so much so that it even seems to me he would have been unable to live without it." (10:7)

Of course, nineteenth century Russia was replete with many deep-thinking and committed members of the *intelligentsiya*, such as the aforementioned Chaadaev, Belinsky, Granovsky, and Herzen.[6] Stepan Trofimovich possesses, it seems, a somewhat different character. The narrator reminds us that he was, ". . . only an imitator compared with such persons." (10:12) He imitated them in *style*, but never in *action*. The fact is, he never *publicly* spoke out against the Tsarist regime. This is the primary reason why, as the narrator reminds us, that Stepan Trofimovich, ". . . had never even been under surveillance." (10:8)

All of this may be partly due to the fact that Stepan Trofimovich does not seem to have any deep-seated convictions at all. As was pointed out to him, he proclaimed to adhere to the liberal value of equality, yet he sold his servant

Fedya ("the convict") to the army in order to pay off a gambling debt. We are also reminded that at the first sign of trouble, after Blum had confiscated his books, he orders an icon lamp to be placed in his room. Stepan Trofimovich is simply playing the role of an *intelligent.*

In fact, his commitment to equality is manifest as more of a psychological weakness than as a strength. As a cosmopolitan democrat he adheres to the concept of equality, a concept he applies to his relationships with his pupils. The narrator explains that Stepan Trofimovich's egalitarian approach to his pupils resulted in the young students taking well to him. The problem, however, is that Stepan Trofimovich lowers himself to their level, rather than the other way around. The narrator writes,

> One must do Stepan Trofimovich justice: he knew how to win his pupil over [Nikolai Vsevolodovich]. The whole secret lay in being a child himself. I [the narrator] was not around then; he was constantly in need of a true friend. He did not hesitate to make a friend of such a small being. . . . More than once he awakened his ten- or eleven-year-old friend at night only to pour out his injured feelings in tears before him, or to reveal some domestic secret to him, not noticing that this was altogether improper. (10:35)

At the end of the day, Stepan Trofimovich fancies himself as an *intelligent* for three fundamental reasons. First, and perhaps most importantly, is the fact that he was entirely devoid of constructive ideas. As any undergraduate college student knows, it is far easier to critique ideas than to construct them. Stepan Trofimovich is intellectually weak. By embracing a critical stance he can wear the cloak of intelligence while not actually possessing the rarer ability to construct ideas and arguments. Secondly, and somewhat more subtly, by speaking out against his own country, Stepan Trofimovich can easily psychologically justify why he is so unappreciated within it. In reality, he is unappreciated because he is utterly devoid of talent. Thirdly, he embraces the egalitarian aspects of an *intelligent* out of a psychological weakness; his embrace of equality allows him to descend to the level of children in the name of social progressiveness.

The Cosmopolitan Father

A child is the center of his own universe. As the child ages, he slowly gains an awareness that there are others with whom he must share that universe. Eventually, his Ptolemaic universe, with him at the center, is replaced with a Copernican universe, in which he is not the center of the universe, but only one of many orbiting objects. The Ptolemaic Stepan Trofimovich never makes that transition. As such, he is an extraordinarily neglectful father. At the opening of the novel we learn that he had abandoned his motherless child, Pyotr Stepanovich, in infancy and had seen him only once in the next twenty years. In fact, as Pyotr first makes his appearance in the novel, Stepan does not immediately recognize him. (10:144) After all, he had not seen him for ten years.

As a child, Pyotr Stepanovich had been sent to a remote village to be raised by several distant aunts. Stepan Trofimovich provided support to his son based upon the profit of the small estate that had belonged to his first wife. Pyotr Stepanovich is set to inherit this small estate upon reaching adulthood. His father is nothing more than a trustee.

As seen above, Stepan Trofimovich is hardly the model of business acumen. Varvara Petrovna must ensure that Pyotr Stepanovich always receives his annual allotment of 1,000 rubles.

Upon completing University studies, Pyotr Stepanovich traveled to Switzerland where he continued to receive his annual allotments. During this period, the written communication between father and son was cold and business-like. Our narrator assures us that the tone of these communications, ". . . looked like those letters of instruction that old-time landowners used to send from the capital to the caretakers appointed to manage their estates." (10:64)

In spite of Varvara Petrovna's help, Stepan Trofimovich still managed the small estate badly, mostly through poor sales and gambling debts. When Pyotr Stepanovich informed his father that he was coming home to collect his inheritance, Stepan Trofimovich states, "I'm now awaiting my poor boy, before whom . . . oh, before whom I am so guilty!" (10:75) He recognizes that he is guilty of squandering his son's inheritance, but his vanity blinds him from seeing his paternal neglect.

Stepan Trofimovich's neglect of his child stems from his own childish nature. He treats his son as any child would treat a friend—as an equal. Indeed, in the midst of one discussion he states, "Pierre, you might express yourself differently with me, is that not so, my friend?" (10:163)

This desire to be equal with his son compels Stepan Trofimovich to read Cherneshevsky's novel *What Is to Be Done?* Rather than reading it with the intention of trying to bridge the gap with his son he, "was studying it with a single purpose, so that in the event of an unquestionable confrontation with the 'screamers,' he would know their methods and arguments beforehand from their own 'catechism,' and being thus prepared, would solemnly refute them all in *her eyes*." (10:238) In essence, he is ready to argue with them on their level. To make matters worse, he is doing this in order to win the approval of Varvara Petrovna—the maternal figure in his life.

Pyotr Stepanovich is understandably resentful. We note, for instance, that after the initial meeting between Pyotr and his father, Pyotr visits his father for the next time only after four days—and this is for the sole purpose of settling the details of the sale of the small estate. As they discuss this, Pyotr Stepanovich accuses his father, "You did not give me drink . . . and sent me off by mail, and here, on top of that, you even robbed me." (10:171) He elaborates later, ". . . he didn't spend a ruble on me all his life, he didn't know me at all till I was sixteen, then he robbed me here, and now he shouts that his heart has ached for me all his life, and poses in front of me like an actor. Really, I'm not Varvara Petrovna, for pity's sake!" (10:240)

Anger is clearly a key characteristic of Pyotr Stepanovich. So is revenge. After having isolated his father's key weakness—his cosmopolitan vanity—

Pyotr Stepanovich begins his verbally demeaning attack upon his father. He tells his father, "Well, brother, I really had a good chuckle over your letters to her [Varvara Petrovna]; shameful and disgusting. But you are all so depraved, so depraved." (10:239) In yet another incident, he publicly reads out a letter written by Stepan Trofimovich, in which he states that he must get married, "for another's sins committed in Switzerland." (10:161) If this were not enough, Pyotr Stepanovich then goes on to state that his father's letters are, ". . . endless and without interruption . . . but do please admit that, though you addressed them to me, you were still writing more for posterity. . . . " (10:162)

By the end of the novel, Stepan Trofimovich realizes that his cosmopolitan vanity has led not only to the destruction of the relationship with his son, but to his own destruction. During one of his last monologues, Stepan refers to Luke 8:32-36 by stating "It is us, us and them, and Petrush . . . et les autres avec lui, and I , perhaps first, at the head, and we will rush, insane and ranging, from the cliffs down into the sea, and all be drowned, and good riddance to us, because that's the most we're fit for. . . ." (10:499)

Why does he feel that he will be running at the head of this crowd of possessed swine? The answer once again involves his vanity or pride. Dostoevsky was, of course, a devout Russian Orthodox Christian. As such, he adhered to the Orthodox belief that the origin of evil can be found at the very dawn of creation with the fall from grace of Lucifer, an angel belonging to one of the highest ranks within the angelic hierarchy. Lucifer led a revolt against God stemming from his own vanity (or pride).[7] Once his revolt had collapsed in defeat, he was expelled from heaven to reside on earth with one third of God's compliment of angels, who also had fallen from grace. They became his demonic allies.

The sin of vanity/pride, an excessively high opinion of self-worth which leads to a feeling of superiority over others combined with a desire for admiration, today stands as the most significant of all the major sins within both the Orthodox and Western Christian churches because it was the sin that led to the creation of evil. Stepan Trofimovich leads the charge of the possessed swine into the ocean because his vanity/pride had made him into the equivalent of the first sinner—Lucifer—who led the other demons operating within the world.

Cosmopolitan Despotism

Dostoevsky does not elaborate upon Stepan Trofimovich's political ideology. We only read that he has a vague commitment to the principle of equality. This is in contrast to the extensive coverage we see dealing with his other cosmopolitan, and rootless, cultural characteristics. For Dostoevsky it is the rootlessness of this rootless egalitarian that is his primary flaw. Tocqueville, a *political* writer, brings us to despotism along a similar route, but focuses upon the political rather than the cultural. Indeed, *Democracy in America*, hinges upon the principle of equality and how it affects every aspect of American life. For Tocqueville, it is *the* principle that explains America. For Tocqueville, it is therefore the principle that must be carefully examined if we are to understand the potential end to democracy in America.

Tocqueville traveled to America in 1831 and, in the course of his nine-month trip, gathered enough material for both Volumes I and II of his enormously influential book, *Democracy in America*, published in 1835 and 1840 respectively. Within this work, Tocqueville wrote admiringly about America and about the "generative fact" for everything within it—equality of conditions.[8] Throughout Volume I, it is the principle of equality that is the ". . . central point at which all my observations came to an end."[9] Through this principle he explains the customs and institutions of democracy as practiced in the United States.

Volume II is of greater importance to us here, for in it Tocqueville describes how the "equality of conditions" affects the way in which Americans think, feel, and behave. Tocqueville begins this volume by arguing that equality naturally creates a mode of thinking which compels Americans, ". . . to seek the reason for things by themselves and in themselves alone. . . ."[10] Each American is proudly self-reliant, relying upon no external authority upon which to base his opinions.[11] Consequently, he withdraws, ". . . narrowly into himself and claims to judge the world from there. . . ."[12] This is the root of what is commonly referred to as American individualism.

For Tocqueville, this individualism is potentially quite problematic for it leads each member of society to become isolated and to withdraw from society. He only concerns himself with family and friends. Tocqueville writes that individualism, ". . . dries up only the source of public virtues; but in the long term it attacks and destroys all the others and will finally be absorbed in selfishness."[13] The selfish citizen displays an exaggerated self-love, relating everything only to his own interests, and preferring himself to all else.[14]

Tocqueville feels that the Americans had devised a brilliant way to combat the evils of excessive individualism. He argues that through free institutions and associations, Americans are able to avoid slipping into a nation dominated by selfish individualists. He concludes, "In democratic countries the science of association is the mother science; the progress of all the others depends on the progress of that one."[15]

In the following section, Tocqueville devotes himself to the "sentiments" brought about by the equality of conditions. Foremost among these is the love of material enjoyments.[16] Equality produces social mobility; the poor desire to become rich, while the rich fear becoming poor.[17] He somewhat humorously notes, "It is a strange thing to see with what ardor Americans pursue well-being and how they show themselves constantly tormented by a vague fear of not having chosen the shortest route that can lead to it."[18] The American is therefore constantly restless and hurrying.

Tocqueville does not rule out the positive aspects of materialism, he is primarily concerned with it in its excessive form. He argues for an, ". . . honest materialism that does not corrupt souls, but softens them and in the end quietly loosens all their tensions."[19] But what makes for this "honest materialism?"

Tocqueville argues that religion is the key to providing this. Religion feeds the desire for the eternal, the immaterial. He writes that, "There is no religion that does not place a man's desires beyond and above earthly goods and that does not naturally raise his soul toward regions much superior to those of the senses."[20]

Interestingly, when religion is destroyed, disastrous things happen. He writes, "When religion is destroyed in a people, doubt takes hold of the highest portions of the intellect and half paralyzes all the others. . . . Such a state cannot fail to enervate souls; it slackens the springs of the will and prepares citizens for servitude."[21] He concludes, "Religious peoples are therefore naturally strong in precisely the spot where democratic peoples are weak [in being overly materialistic]; this makes very visible how important it is that men keep to their religion when becoming equal."[22]

This then sets the stage for part IV of Volume II in which Tocqueville describes how the neglect of religion and public virtue (as exercised through associations) can drive the citizens of a democracy, ". . . by a longer, more secret, but surer path toward servitude."[23] As materialists, the citizens of democracy fear public disorder. The greatest threat to their material enjoyments is such disorder. In order to preserve public order and property, citizens of a democracy will endow the central government with tasks they no longer want to do themselves. He writes, "Not only do they not naturally have the taste to occupy themselves with the public, but often they lack the time to do it. Private life is so active in democratic times, so agitated, so filled with desires and work, that hardly any energy or leisure remains to each man for political life."[24]

Tocqueville believes this to be disastrous. He argues that every central government adores uniformity. He writes, ". . . uniformity spares it the examination of an infinity of details with which it would have to occupy itself if it were necessary to make a rule for men, instead of making all men pass indiscriminately under the same rule."[25]

It is within this context that Tocqueville writes what is, for our purposes, the most important passage of the book. He writes that,

> . . . an immense tutelary power is elevated . . . it seeks only to keep them fixed irrevocably in childhood; it likes citizens to enjoy themselves provided that they think only of enjoying themselves. It willingly works for their happiness; but it wants to be the unique agent and sole arbiter of that; it provides for their security, foresees and secures their needs, facilitates their pleasures, conducts their principal affairs, directs their industry, regulates their estates, divides their inheritances; can it not take away from them entirely the trouble of thinking and the pain of living? . . . it covers its surface with a network of small, complicated, painstaking, uniform rules through which the most original minds and the most vigorous souls cannot clear a way to surpass the crowd; it does not break wills, but it constantly opposes itself to one's acting; it does not destroy, it prevents things from being born; it does not tyrannize, it hinders, compromises, enervates, extinguishes, dazes, and finally reduces each nation to being nothing more than a herd of timid and industrious animals of which the government is the shepherd.[26]

Rootless democracy, the political regime based upon the principle of tradition-less equality, does not end in a great cataclysmic revolution. It ends mildly, gradually, with the complicity of the citizens.

For the reader of *The Demons*, it is hardly a conceptual stretch to think of Stepan Trofimovich as the democratic man. He is an unreflective man of limited horizons, socially isolated, concerned only with his material enjoyments and his own vanity. As a cosmopolitan man, he is without religion or (real) public virtue. If Dostoevsky agrees with Tocqueville in that a democracy without these two items leads to democratic despotism, we should expect that the creation of Stepan Trofimovich—Pyotr Stepanovich—should be a democratic despot. This is precisely what we find.

Shigalyovism

Through the character of Pyotr Stepanovich, we see Dostoevsky's concern about the product of rootless egalitarianism—the democratic despot. Strikingly we do not even learn about this until two thirds of the way through the novel. Through innuendo, the reader is led to believe, up to that point, that Pyotr Stepanovich intends to lead a socialist revolution. After a few drinks, however, he reveals his true intentions.

Having chased down Nikolai Vsevolodovich after his abrupt departure from a revolutionary meeting, Pyotr Stepanovich blurts out, "I'm for Shigalyovism." (10:322) Earlier in the book, Shigalyov had put forward an ideology in which mankind is divided into two unequal parts. One tenth of the population is granted complete freedom and unlimited power over the remaining nine tenths.[27] The powerless nine tenths become herd-like. Through their unlimited obedience, they attain to a certain primeval innocence—an earthly paradise. (10:312) The minority leadership ensures that they stay this way.

Somewhat reminiscent of Tocqueville, he argues that public virtue must be quashed through the cultivation of extreme individualism. Pyotr states that one or two generations of "mean depravity" are necessary to turn men into, ". . . vile, cowardly, cruel, vain slime." (10:325) He continues,

> We'll extinguish desire: we'll get drinking, gossip, denunciation going; we'll get unheard-of depravity going; we'll stifle every genius in infancy. Everything reduced to a common denominator, complete equality . . . complete obedience, complete impersonality, but once every thirty years Shigalyov gets a convulsion going, and they all suddenly start consuming each other, up to a certain point, simply so as not to be bored. Boredom is an aristocratic sensation; in Shigalyovism there will be no desires. Desire and suffering are for us; and for the slaves—Shigalyovism. (10:323)

Pyotr concludes: "Only one thing is lacking in the world: obedience." (10:323)

Much like Tocqueville's description of the effects of democracy on the arts, Pyotr's explains of Shigalyovism,

> First, the level of education, science, and talents is lowered. A high level of science and talents is accessible only to higher abilities—no need for higher abilities! Higher abilities have always seized power and become despots. Higher abilities cannot fail to be despots and have always corrupted rather than been of use; they are to be banished or executed. Cicero's tongue is cut off, Copernicus's eyes are put out, Shakespeare is stoned. (10:322)

Importantly, Dostoevsky adds two additional components to the evolution of rootless equality that proved to be quite prophetic for Russia: spying and violence. Pyotr explains, "He [Shigalyov] advocates for each member of society to watch the others and they are obliged to inform on each other. Each belongs to all, and all to each. They are all slaves and equal in their slavery. Slander and murder in extreme cases, but above all—equality." (10:322) This is augmented by, ". . . a bit of 'fresh blood!' to boot, for the sake of habit." (10:325)

In claiming to be a socialist, Pyotr Stepanovich is a fraud. He even admits that he is a "swindler" not a "socialist." (10:324) Much like Tocqueville's depraved democracy, he claims to be something he is not. He proclaims to act in the name of the people, but he is only out for personal power.

Reforming the Cosmopolitan

In *The Demons* Dostoevsky portrays the dangers of cosmopolitanism without providing for an escape from its influences. Frustrating for many modern readers, it is up to the individual reader to put the pieces together in order to figure out what Dostoevsky is saying about the means to cope with the negative aspects of cosmopolitan culture. The ultimate demise of Stepan Trofimovich is particularly perplexing. What is Dostoevsky attempting to say with this somewhat ambiguous and unsatisfactory end for the novel's main character?

We may again turn to Tocqueville for help in this matter, for if Stepan Trofimovich is meant to personify cosmopolitan democracy, how does Tocqueville suggest that a cosmopolitan democracy, once it has lost its roots, will save itself? Tocqueville is not optimistic about such a situation. He writes,

> It is in fact difficult to conceive how men who have entirely renounced the habit of directing themselves could succeed at choosing well those who will lead them; and one will not make anyone believe that a liberal, energetic, and wise government can ever issue from the suffrage of a people of servants.[28]

The ultimate demise of Stepan Trofimovich illustrates that Dostoevsky seems to agree with this rather sobering assessment of the lost democratic man. In the chapters entitled, "The Fete, Part I" and "The Last Quest of Stepan Trofimovich," we see how Stepan Trofimovich cracks under the strain of twenty years of cosmopolitan life.[29] The pressures of his unsatisfied vanity, unrealized love for Varvara, his revolutionary son (and guilt over neglecting him), and the confiscation of his books by the authorities seems to have pushed him into realizing that he must change his life radically. Freed from his cosmopolitan moorings, however, he has no clue as to where he must go or what he must do.

He begins this process by making a public denunciation of cosmopolitanism at the long-awaited fete. In a vain and ridiculous speech Stepan Trofimovich attacks the message of the revolutionary tracts that had been circulating through town by claiming that, "The whole mystery of their effect lies—in their stupidity." (10:371) He then continues,

> Messieurs, the last word in this matter is all-forgiveness. . . . Only one thing has happened: the displacing of purposes, the replacing of one beauty by another! The whole perplexity lies in just what is more beautiful: Shakespeare or boots, Raphael or petroleum? . . . I proclaim that Shakespeare and Raphael are higher than the emancipation of the serfs, higher than nationality, higher than socialism, higher than the younger generation, higher than chemistry, higher than almost all mankind, for they are already the fruit, the real fruit of all mankind, and maybe the highest fruit there ever may be! . . . And do you know, do you know that mankind can live without the Englishman, it can live without Germany, it can definitely live without the Russian, it can live without science, without bread, and it only cannot live without beauty, for then there would be nothing at all to do in the world! The whole secret of history is here! (10:372-373)

The speech itself is made in a state of semi-delirium. As events unfold, he becomes more and more delirious. After the speech, he retreats to a locked room to write a letter to Darya Pavlovna in which he states, ". . . I am leaving this town forever, whither I do not know." (10:377)[30] In essence, he knows he must escape, he simply does not know how—or for what purpose. At one point he says that he wants to "seek Russia." However, he never returns to this idea. At another moment he just wants to take the "high road" (i.e., just go walking). At yet another point he wants to travel under "the banner of a great idea." We never really learn what this "great idea" is.

What is truly propelling Stepan Trofimovich is a psychological impulse. The narrator senses this and states, "There was something proud here that he admired in spite of everything." (10:480) Indeed, the narrator feels that this adventure is somehow "beautiful" and "vindictively amorous." (10:480) In essence, his journey is more a flight from the intolerable under the guise of a vanity-laden quest.

What is clear is that this trip is, in the words of the narrator, "insane." Indeed, the picture painted of him as he embarks upon this journey is ridiculous. Not knowing where to go, he is also completely ill prepared for any sort of trip in the out-of-doors. We see him set off with an umbrella, a bag, and a walking stick (with only two hands!). On top of this, he is in a delirium.

Through the chaos of this trip, the reader gradually realizes that Stepan Trofimovich's end-goal is one of Christian salvation. The first hint of this occurs when he encounters his first human contact after embarking upon this quest. Upon seeing Liza and Mavriky, he states, "We are all unhappy, but we must forgive them all [those that burnt down the town]. Let us forgive, Liza . . . and be free forever." (10:411)

The theme of a Christian journey persists as he continues along his trip. In the town of his first stop (Khatovo) he meets up with a Bible seller, Sofya Matveevna Ulitin, who promises to take him to Spasov—a town whose name clearly derives from the Russian verb "to save." Sofya Matveevna ends up being his spiritual confident on this wandering quest to be saved.

Significantly, he never reaches Spasov. While awaiting a ferry at Ustyevo, the river-port way station on the way to Spasov, he falls ill and, in the midst of his delirium, comes to the conclusion that he has played a demonic role for Russian society. It is at this point, shortly before his death, that he draws the analogy between his life and the passage in Luke 8:32-36. He concludes that *he* is the possessed swine who leads the rest in their mad dash into the sea.

Although his redemption through God is incomplete, if not simply ridiculous, Stepan Trofimovich's return to religion, and God's love, allows him to declare his love for Varvara Petrovna. Upon declaring their mutual love for each other, Stepan Trofimovich dies.

Dostoevsky implies through this ending that a true redemption for any such person as Stepan Trofimovich is exceedingly difficult, if not impossible. The first problem is one of age. With age, one becomes more set in one's habits. A similar figure from *The Idiot*, Afanasy Ivanovich, is described by Dostoevsky as being, ". . . a man of about fifty, he was to a great degree fixed and firm in his ways." (8:37) In *The Demons*, Stepan Trofimovich is fifty-three years old.

The second problem is that he is ill prepared intellectually to deal with anything that is not cosmopolitan. He has spent his entire life focused upon esoteric, scholarly topics or radical causes. At fifty-three years of age, he comes to the sudden conclusion that he has been on the wrong path. He thrashes about to find a new path—nature, the Russian people, a quest, Christian love and forgiveness. For Dostoevsky, he has no foundation in that which is necessary to save him in a Christian sense. In Ustyevo, he tells Sofya that he has not read the Bible in at least thirty years. He then ridiculously decides that he will preach the gospel to the people anyway. He states, "I will expound it to them. . . . In expounding it orally, it is possible to correct the mistakes of this remarkable book. . . ." (10:491)

This is complicated by the fact that there is no one in town that can effectively guide him to Christian redemption—which is what Dostoevsky feels is necessary for salvation. By the end of the novel, it seems that every inhabitant of the town of Skvoreshniki is "possessed" by demons. The one character who seems free from possession, Darya Pavlovna (Shatova), is unable to connect with Stepan Trofimovich as a result of the failed "engagement." Even the local "blessed man" and prophet, Semyon Yakovlevich, who had been living with the merchant Sevostyanov, seems possessed. Once Stepan Trofimovich is outside of the possessed town, a glimmer of hope is provided by Sofya Matveevna, the

Bible seller. She can lead Stepan Trofimovich to salvation (Spasov).[31] Unfortunately, it is too little, too late.

The Violence of Cosmopolitanism

At its worst, rootless or cosmopolitan, democracy is vain, unreflective, uninspiring, and childish. For Dostoevsky, Stepan Trofimovich is the cosmopolitan democratic man. As a cosmopolitan democrat, he lacks roots, traditions, and religion. Toward the end of this novel, Stepan appears to understand this. As we saw above in his speech to the fete, he proclaims that the progressive political forces who push for democracy are creating an ugly world—a world devoid of meaning and beauty.

For Dostoevsky, democracy brings equality and freedom. It does not naturally bring beauty or tradition. The danger of cosmopolitanism is precisely that it destroys the beauty and tradition that can, paradoxically, safeguard the democratic values of equality and freedom. What is left is the extreme equality of Shigalyovism combined with the value-less nihilism of Nikolai Vsevolodovich.

It cannot go without mentioning at this point that one significant, seemingly dramatic, difference between Dostoevsky and Tocqueville appears as we consider *how* a cosmopolitan democracy descends into despotism. Tocqueville felt that democracy in America would fade away gently and unnoticeably, while Dostoevsky felt that the product of the democratic man would do it violently—through terrorism. How can we explain the difference?

In chapter 12 of Volume II, Tocqueville writes the following passage which helps to explain how one aspect of the understanding of equality in the European Russia of Dostoevsky differs from that of America:

> There are people in Europe who, confusing the diverse attributes of the sexes, intend to make man and woman into beings not only equal, but alike. They give both the same function, impose the same duties on them, and accord them the same rights; they mix them in all things—labors, pleasures, affairs. One can easily conceive that in thus striving to equalize one sex with the other, one degrades them both; and that from this coarse mixture of nature's works, only weak men and disreputable women can ever emerge. . . . This is not the way Americans have understood the kind of democratic equality that can be established between woman and man . . . they have wanted them both to march at an equal pace but on ever different paths.[32]

Because his book is about American democracy, Tocqueville did not elaborate upon the consequences of gender "alikeness." It did not exist in America in 1831 and thus did not merit Tocqueville's time and effort.

It does however play a role for Dostoevsky's European Russia. Indeed, as mentioned above, Stepan Trofimovich professes an admiration of George Sand, a woman famous for wearing men's clothes and smoking in public. More importantly, Stepan Trofimovich should certainly be considered a "weak man." His first wife, the mother of Pyotr Stepanovich is certainly "disreputable" (recall that the marriage ended due to certain "delicate" reasons). (10:11) The product of this androgynous union is the terrorist, Pyotr Stepanovich.

With regard to the creation of the most violent character of *The Demons*, Nikolai Vsevolodovich, the gender-bending habits of Varvara Petrovna seem to be of prime concern. In becoming man-like, Varvara Petrovna loses her maternal abilities and deprives her son of the first and most basic of human loves. This maternal neglect has serious psychological effects upon Nikolai which ultimately results in his "self-death" and subsequent nihilistic violence. It is to this point that we devote our fourth chapter—entitled, "The Psychology of Cosmopolitanism."

Notes

1. Dostoevsky does not mention the word cosmopolitan in *The Demons*. It seems likely that Dostoevsky may very well have realized that the term "cosmopolitan" normally has quite positive connotations. Rather than confuse the reader by associating the neurotic characters of *The Demons* with this term, he very likely opted simply not to use the term in the novel.

2. See Jean-Jacques Rousseau, *Julie or the New Heloise: Letters of Two Lovers Who Live in a Small Town at the Foot of the Alps*, trans. Philip Steward and Jean Vache (London: University Press of New England, 1997).

3. Reference notes here are to F. M. Dostoevsky, *Besy*, Volumes 10 and 11 (Leningrad: Nauka, 1974). Ultimately, I am responsible for the translation from Russian to English although I am heavily indebted to two previous translations that I found to be enormously helpful in this task: Fyodor Dostoevsky, *Demons*, trans. Richard Pevear and Larissa Volokhonsky (New York: Vintage Books, 1994) and Fyodor Dostoevsky, *Devils*, trans. Michael Katz (New York: Oxford University Press, 1992).

4. Tibor Szamuely, *The Russian Tradition* (London: Fontana Books, 1988): 191. Perhaps the classic statement of the Russian intelligentsia is Marc Raeff's *Origins of the Russian Intelligentsia* (New York: HBJ Book, 1966).

5. Of course, the Russian intelligentsia defined equality in a variety of different ways. The socialists or radicals tended to focus on the material aspects of equality, while those who chose to emphasize social and political equality (in the Western sense) considered themselves to be Westernizers.

6. Dostoevsky intended for the character of Stepan Trofimovich to represent Granovsky. See Joseph Frank, *Dostoevsky: The Miraculous Years, 1865-1871* (Princeton, N.J.: Princeton University Press, 1995): 461-463.

7. Christian theology has, in essence, merged the sins of vanity and pride into one of the seven deadly sins.

8. Alexis de Tocqueville, *Democracy in America*, trans. Harvey C. Mansfield and Delba Winthrope (Chicago: University of Chicago Press, 2002): 3.

9. Alexis de Tocqueville, *Democracy in America*, 3.

10. Alexis de Tocqueville, *Democracy in America*, 403.

11. Tocqueville does grant that there is one external authority that the citizen of the United States takes into account—that is that of public opinion at large.

12. Alexis de Tocqueville, *Democracy in America*, 404.

13. Alexis de Tocqueville, *Democracy in America*, 483.

14. Alexis de Tocqueville, *Democracy in America,* 482.
15. Alexis de Tocqueville, *Democracy in America,* 492.
16. Alexis de Tocqueville, *Democracy in America,* 419.
17. Alexis de Tocqueville, *Democracy in America,* 507.
18. Alexis de Tocqueville, *Democracy in America,* 511.
19. Alexis de Tocqueville, *Democracy in America,* 509.
20. Alexis de Tocqueville, *Democracy in America,* 419.
21. Alexis de Tocqueville, *Democracy in America,* 418.
22. Alexis de Tocqueville, *Democracy in America,* 419.
23. Alexis de Tocqueville, *Democracy in America,* 640.
24. Alexis de Tocqueville, *Democracy in America,* 643.
25. Alexis de Tocqueville, *Democracy in America,* 645.
26. Alexis de Tocqueville, *Democracy in America,* 663.
27. Joseph Frank points out that, "Shigalev, in Dostoevsky's notes, is first called Zaitsev; and one of his physical features—his long ears—is probably derived from an adjective (*visloykhii*, lop-eared) applied to Zaitsev and Pisarev by Saltykov-Shchedrin during the 'Schism among the Nihilists' controversy." See Joseph Frank, *Dostoevsky: The Miraculous Years, 1865-1871* (Princeton, N.J.: Princeton University Press, 1995): 449.
28. Alexis de Tocqueville, *Democracy in America,* 665.
29. The word *stranstvovanie* derives from the verb *stranstvovat'* meaning to travel in such a way as to constantly change the place where one will stay. Different translations of this have appeared in English versions of *The Demons*: wandering (Garnett), journey (Katz), pilgrimage (Magarshack), peregrination (Pevear/Volokhonsky). There is an end goal to the journey, but the means to achieve it are unclear. In this sense, "quest" seems a better translation. My thanks to Dr. Katya Vladimirov for pointing this out.
30. Both Stepan and Nikolai seem to recognize that Darya is the only non-possessed character in town—and thus the only one that could conceivably help them. Unlike Sonya in *Crime and Punishment* and Zosima in *The Brothers Karamazov*, circumstances keep her from actually helping.
31. In fact, the two most famous figures of Dostoesky's great novels Raskolnikov and Alyosha, both had spiritual advisors (Sonya and Zosima). Through these two advisors, both these figures were "saved."
32. Alexis de Tocqueville, *Democracy in America,* 574.

Chapter 4
The Psychology of Cosmopolitanism

One of the most popular images of demons today can be found in the 1973 blockbuster movie, *The Exorcist*. In this film, a young girl is possessed by a demon. The supernatural powers she exercises under his demonic influence are frightening. She can telepathically move heavy furniture and shake the room at will. She can spin her head, spout green vomit, and speak with a sinister voice. Her language and behavior are vulgar, designed to elicit fear and rage. She is, in essence, a hideous monster.

The Exorcist was the top grossing movie of 1973 due to its ability to combine virtually all of the component parts of a sensational movie: violence, vulgarity, a hint of sex, blasphemy, and of course, intense horror—all in one character. Not only did this film provide an image of a violent, vulgar villain (a formula common heretofore), but one that was literally *evil*. This villain was no mere Frankenstein or Dracula, but the devil himself. Here was a villain who could actually possess his victim and rob him of his soul. It is perhaps not surprising that this film remains a popular film as well as a part of the student lore at Georgetown University, the location of the filming of many of its scenes and the alma mater of the author of the novel upon which the film was based, William Peter Blatty.

For Dostoevsky, this monstrous image of the devil is for the uneducated and unreflective. The "demons" that he presents to us in *The Demons* are much more subtle. In fact, they are banal. As has already been discussed, Dostoevsky intended to portray the creation of the novel's chief political demon, Pyotr Stepanovich, not as the result of some mysterious or mystical possession, but as the ideological extension of his father, the cosmopolitan figure of Stepan Trofimovich Verkhovensky. Nikolai Vsevolodovich Stavrogin, however, is only partially created by Stepan Trofimovich. He has another major influence—his mother, Varvara Petrovna Stavrogina. It is to this relationship that we must now turn to understand the creation of this rather different, and intriguing, demon. Indeed, this is the character that is meant to portray the purest type of demon—a man who has rejected all ideals and values and who is devoid of all human emotion. For Dostoevsky, a demon is not a monster that spits green vomit or spins his head around on his shoulders, but simply a man who rejects ideals and values. For him, a demon is simply a nihilist, and Nikolai Vsevolodovich represents its most advanced type.

The Wise Serpent

It is in chapter 3 of part I of *The Demons* that Dostoevsky provides the first important clue that paves the way to an understanding of Nikolai Vsevolodovich. In an effort to learn more about her son, Varvara Petrovna calls together a small group of acquaintances in order to help her understand Nikolai's unpredictable behavior. In the midst of this interview, the most prolific gossipmonger in the book, Liputin, blurts out that the town drunk, Lebyadkin, once described Nikolai as a "wise serpent." (10:83) At first, the reader is tempted to disregard this description as the meaningless words of a drunkard as related by a scandalmonger. The perceptive reader, however, is presented, two chapters later, with a chapter heading which reads "Wise Serpent." Surely, there must be something to this.

Indeed there is. The exact words that Lebyadkin uses are "*premudryi zmij*" ["wise serpent"]. These words are somewhat troubling to the average reader for two reasons. The first is obvious—serpents are usually not described as "wise." They are usually perceived as being devious, clever, even evil, but not wise. Secondly, the word "serpent" ("*zmij*") is not commonly used in the daily Russian language. Just as in English, it is found primarily in either the Bible or in children's fairy tales. It is quite similar to the Russian word for "snake" ("*zmej*"), differing only in the second to last letter. Why does Dostoevsky have Lebyadkin use this word?

For a church-going Russian speaker, the answer to this question is fairly clear-cut. The words "*premudryi zmij*" are derived from the Old Church Slavonic words found in the beginning of chapter 3 of Genesis, where we find the story of Adam and Eve in the Garden of Eden. The problem here is found in the fact that Lebyadkin misunderstands the words as they are written and spoken in Old Church Slavonic, a proto-Slavonic language similar to Russian. According to the old text, the serpent that tempted Eve is referred to as a "*mudr'jashji zmij.*" The word "*mudr'jashji*" sounds quite similar to the Russian word of "*premudryi,*" which means "wise." This similarity is deceiving; the most accurate translation of this word is "clever" or "subtle." In fact, when the Russian-language edition of the Bible was published in 1876, the Russian words used to depict this were, "*khitri zmei.*" The word "*khitri*" is usually translated into English as "clever" or "tricky."

This error made on the part of this drunkard, is important in providing two possible approaches to Nikolai Vsevolodovich. He is either a "wise" serpent or he is a "tricky" serpent. A wise individual is usually perceived as having the capability to determine what is right, true, or of lasting value. There are characters in the book that perceive Nikolai Vsevolodovich in this light. In fact, Dostoevsky writes that, "All our ladies went crazy over the new visitor [Nikolai]. They sharply divided themselves into two parties—one party adored him, the other hated him to the point of blood vengeance; but both groups were crazy." (10:37) Those that hated him perceived him as more "tricky" than "wise."

Perhaps there is yet another explanation. Is it possible to be both "tricky" and "wise"? This is where we must consider the "serpent." The serpent of the Garden of Eden was certainly "tricky," but he was also "wise" insofar as he was able to penetrate to the core truth of Eve's nature. He discerned in her a desire to possess God-like knowledge. Using this truth, he cleverly tricked her into breaking God's law. Importantly, no direct clue is given as to *why* the serpent so wanted to corrupt Eve. We can only assume that he also sought to be God-like; by convincing Eve to break with God's law, he was exercising God-like power.

There are only two types of Biblical figures that encourage humans to break with God's law—the serpent of the Garden of Eden and demons. According to Christian tradition, demons are divine beings that, through sin, descended from their heavenly homes to the netherworld. In the New Testament, they are seen as tempters. Perhaps the most famous appearance of such a tempter in the Bible is found in Matthew 4, "Temptation of Christ," in which Christ is offered a variety of desirable objects (food, freedom from the fear of death, and power) if only he would worship Satan. He refuses and casts the devil away. From this point onward, Christ has the power to cure demoniacs who are often characterized as being blind, dumb, epileptic, and mad. In Luke 9:1, Christ's disciples are given the power to exorcise demons, and in Acts 19 we read of Paul exorcising demons.

Importantly, both the serpent of the Garden of Eden and demons often convince individuals to deviate from God's law by appealing to human pride and vanity. It is no coincidence that, as we saw in chapter 3, it is Stepan Trofimovich's vanity that compels him to embrace cosmopolitanism. This vanity and cosmopolitanism are exaggerated in his son, Pyotr Stepanovich, who emerges not only as an arrogant nihilist, but as an advocate of an extreme version of cosmopolitan egalitarianism. In essence, he is a demon who leads other demons in committing worldly mischief.

Similarly, the source of Nikolai Vsevolodovich's "wise/tricky" nature is found in his vain mother—Varvara Petrovna. However, unlike the vain Stepan Trofimovich, she does not embrace any particular ideology—she is simply vain. Predictably, Nikolai does not embrace an ideology either. He stands only for himself, without restrictions of any sort. He is the very embodiment of individual nihilistic freedom without the constraints of a political ideology or of human conscience. As we will see, it is an ethic that seems enormously useful to a terrorist like Pyotr Stepanovich.

In this way, Dostoevsky presents to us two demons: Pyotr Stepanovich and Nikolai Vsevolodovich. The key difference between the two characters involves more than the fact that one is political while the other is not. Like Pyotr Stepanovich, Nikolai Vsevolodovich feels a deep sense of humiliation and rage. Yet there is something more intense about Nikolai's rage. Why is this?

As mentioned earlier, Nikolai Vsevolodovich is emotionally dead as a result of the cosmopolitan behavior of his mother.[1] As a cosmopolitan, Varvara Petrovna's vanity, combined with her lack of sentiment, compels her to focus only upon herself and to neglect her only son. Nikolai was thus deprived of the *first* and *most basic* of human loves. This maternal neglect has serious psychological effects upon Nikolai that ultimately results in his emotional "self-death." This, in turn, leads him to commit a series of violent attacks, which are designed to test his "moral sensuousness." To state it in the language of modern day psychologists, Nikolai Vsevolodovich is a self-dead individual who continually tests his "deadness" by committing outrages. In not feeling any remorse, he is motivated to escalate his attacks with the hope of feeling some remorse as a result of the new, intensified attack. In other words, upon completing a violent act, he finds himself feeling disappointed to learn that he still feels nothing. He then intensifies the level of violence to the next level.

The Vain Widow

Varvara Petrovna's cosmopolitanism is quite different from that of Stepan Trofimovich. While she shares his vanity and artificiality, she does not adhere to a cosmopolitan ideology. She has no ideology. All she has is her vanity.

Vanity is a type of extreme pride. It is not a form of pride that simply takes satisfaction or delight in ones own successes. By and large, this type of pride is seen as socially redeeming, perhaps even virtuous. Vanity as a form of pride is not arrogance either. This sort of pride is usually defined as an excessively high opinion of one's own importance which gives rise to an attitude of superiority over others. The behavior of such people is often perceived as overbearing. Individuals who are proud feel entitled to receive the appropriately high levels of respect, based upon their perceived self-worth.

As we see with Stepan Trofimovich, vanity is a sentiment in which self-conceit is combined with a desire for admiration. Varvara Petrovna also manifests this somewhat negative trait throughout the novel. As a vain provincial woman she is primarily concerned with the approval of others in her community—particularly the town's social elite. She wants to be associated with all the correct people and be able to say all the correct things at the appropriate time. In one portion of the novel, Dostoevsky depicts an intricately planned fete at which both Varvara Petrovna and Yulia Lembke invest enormous amounts of energy. At one point, Varvara Petrovna even muses that she could throw her own fete after Lembke's so that, ". . . everyone could convince themselves as to whose house was better, and who knew better how to receive and how to give a ball with greater taste." (10:261) Although this never happens, this message is clear—she is preoccupied with the impressions of others.

Varvara Petrovna's vanity is also clearly displayed in a fascinating exchange revolving around the cosmopolitan figure of Karmazinov. The reader will recall that Stepan Trofimovich flies into frenzy when he hears that Varvara is concerned that the writer Karmazinov might not pay her a visit. Indeed, he complains about letters written to him by Varvara that betrayed her "vain and ambitious" concern that the great writer would fail to call upon her.

The Vanity of the Unloved

As a vain woman, Varvara Petrovna desires the approval of those around her. As events unfold, however, it quickly emerges that it is not simply approval that Varvara seeks, but love. This desire to be loved is driven by her belief that she possesses characteristics that make her unloved and unlovable.

Varvara Petrovna is described as an unattractive and stupid woman. The narrator describes her as a tall, yellow, bony woman, ". . . with an extremely long face, which looked somewhat horse like." (10:18) She is also somewhat dim. At one point she decides to read prohibited newspapers, magazines, and revolutionary manifestoes from abroad, but this ". . . only made her head spin." (10:20)

This is capped by the fact that her devoted friend, Stepan Trofimovich, not only does not love her but seems incapable of loving her. As was seen in the previous chapter, he is simply a self-absorbed man-child. Because she seeks the company of an equal, this creates seemingly contradictory feelings in her. At the very beginning of the novel, the narrator writes, "In reality, Varvara Petrovna undoubtedly and quite frequently hated him; but there was one thing he failed to notice in her to the very end, that for her he finally became her son, her creation, the flesh of her flesh." (10:16) This is, of course, a ridiculous relationship. But it explains why Varvara bore, ". . . an unbearable love for him [which] lay hidden in her, in the midst of constant hatred, jealousy, and contempt. . . ." (10:16)

Indeed, as his "mother," she initially attempted to mold him into her ideal image. After twenty-two years of knowing each other, Varvara took him to St. Petersburg to find out about a new political movement with the hope that this would rejuvenate him. She stated that she was even willing to found a magazine for him. When that trip did not result in a societal success, she fruitlessly sent him abroad for rejuvenation. He wrote letters to her which, ". . . consisted of nothing but outpourings of the most genuine love for his absent friend and were literally wet with the tears of separation." (10:25-26) He quickly came rushing back to her.

Just as a mother would for her son, she provides basic sustenance and lodging for him. Throughout the novel, however, appear signs that her intentions are not always maternal. The narrator writes, "She herself even invented a costume for him, which he wore for the rest of his life . . . along with shoulder-length hair." (10:19) This outfit was meant to resemble a portrait she had fallen in love with as a young girl, a portrait of the nineteenth century Russian poet N. V. Kukolnik. It is simply unclear what she was trying to achieve by dressing him in this way. Was she simply acting upon maternal feelings or was she attempting to create a romantic lover in the form of a poet?

Obviously, this unnatural relationship, supported as it was by such contradictory feelings on the part of Varvara Petrovna, was bound to change. Indeed, as the novel progresses, this maternalism becomes increasingly despotic. In one classic harangue, she complains, "By the way, since when have you been wearing a red necktie? . . . And are you exercising?" (10:48) Upon receiving unsatisfactory responses, she declares, "Now you are going to walk not four but six miles a day! You've gotten slack, terribly, ter-ribly! You're not just old, you're decrepit. . . ." (10:48)

In order to control her man-child, Varvara Petrovna does not rely solely upon nagging, but deploys other, subtler, means. The narrator reminds us that she carefully sorts and files away all of the many letters that Stepan Trofimovich sends to her in a special drawer. She perversely wallows in these letters, arming her frustrated ire against him.

Once again, this conflicted behavior stems from her frustrated and unrequited desire to be loved by this "fifty-year-old infant." Stepan Trofimovich shares this desire to be loved. As seen earlier, his adherence to cosmopolitanism is motivated by vanity. Thus, this relationship of two self-absorbed, emotionally needy people, is mutually frustrating. The manifestation of this behavior in Stepan is different than what we see in Varvara. He does not lash out verbally, but on some occasions, just after meeting with her, he would suddenly jump up from the sofa and start pounding on the wall with his fists. (10:12)

Two incidents are recounted that illustrate the growth of this frustration. The first incident involves the visit of a Baron from St. Petersburg and Varvara's intention to put Stepan Trofimovich "on display." In the midst of the discussion about the liberation of the serfs with the Baron, Stepan shouts out, "Hurrah!" After the eventual departure of the Baron, Varvara Petrovna turns to Stepan and informs him that she will never forgive him for this outburst.

How else to interpret Varvara Petrovna's anger but to see Stepan's exclamation of "Hurrah!" as an indication of his self-absorption and childishness? After all, only a child shouts "Hurrah" in such a manner. She is frustrated that after all the years of formation, he remains a child who cannot love her as she would like.

Yet another incident follows the death of Varvara Petrovna's husband. Stepan Trofimovich, in the midst of consoling her, comes to the conclusion that Varvara is expecting him to propose marriage to her. Once she figures this out, she again confronts him by stating, "I will never forgive you for that!" She knows that he is only interested in marrying out of obligation—not that he loves her. She wants him to love her as a man for a woman—not a child simply doing what his mother would expect him to do.

It is Varvara Petrovna's resentment at not being loved by Stepan Trofimovich that motivates her frustrated despotism toward him. Stepan is aware that he is her "galley slave," but he remains unaware of the source of this despotism until the very end of the novel. Stepan, however, is not the only target of her resentment. At one point, Lizaveta Nikolaevna notes that Varvara, "is despotic with everyone. . . ." (10:97) In yet another moment of insightfulness,

Praskovya Ivanovna proclaims to Varvara, "We have had enough of your despotism! . . . They say, whether it's true or not, that you have the whole town marching to your orders, but now it seems your time has come!" (10:131)

It is precisely this resentful despotism that pushes Varvara to pressure Stepan to marry Darya Pavlovna (Dasha) earlier in the novel. Not only is she concerned about her social standing, and the damage to it that may ensue if her son marries the lowly Dasha (rather than the well-to-do Lizaveta), but by forcing the two to marry she is lashing out at two individuals that she paradoxically values and loves. She feels resentment toward them because she feels unloved by them.

It cannot be denied that this mix of emotions causes her to be somewhat contradictory in her actions. In her attempt to convince Dasha to marry Stepan Trofimovich, she describes him by saying that, ". . . he is light-minded, irresolute, cruel, and egoist, with base habits, but you will value him, first of all, because there are much worse." (10:56) She continues, "Stop, wait, there's more. He's an old granny—but so much the better for you. A pitiful old granny, by the way; it's not worthwhile for a woman to love him. But it is worthwhile loving him for his defenselessness, and you will love him for his defenselessness. Do you understand me? Do you?" (10:57) It is almost as if her vanity is pushing her to do one thing, while her hidden love for Stepan is pushing her to do quite another.

It is only at the end of the novel that this frustrated love-hate dynamic between Varvara and Stepan changes. This is achieved through a shattering of Stepan's vanity. Stepan abandons his cosmopolitan vanities and returns to the Russian people and attempts to embrace religion (among other things). Once this is accomplished, he is able to declare his love for Varvara, just three days before his death. This brings Varvara around to admitting (as much as vanity will allow) her long-standing love for him by stating, "Twenty years are gone, there is no bringing them back; I too am a fool." (10:502)

The Vanity of Hal's Mother

Varvara's love for her son is equally as conflicted. She clearly loves him, yet her vanity interferes with the appropriate demonstration of it. With Stepan Trofimovich, her vanity leads to despotic behavior, with her son it leads to a silent distance. The narrator writes, "The boy knew that his mother loved him very much, but he hardly had much love for her. She spoke little to him and rarely interfered in his affairs . . . the whole business of education and moral development, his mother fully entrusted to Stepan Trofimovich." (10:35) The tragedy here is that Varvara's desire to be admired by her son kept her at a significant distance from him.

Dostoevsky tells us very little about the early childhood of Nikolai Vsevolodovich. We learn that he attends University in St. Petersburg after having been tutored by Stepan Trofimovich. After graduation he went into the army. When he returns from the military he begins to frequent places of ill repute with associates of similar reputation. Here he leads a riotous life by gambling, drinking, and brawling. His behavior is also erratic. Varvara Petrovna had heard of, "... some beastly behavior towards a lady of good society with whom he had had a liaison and whom he afterwards publicly insulted." (10:36) He seemed to derive pleasure out of causing discomfort to others.

It is at this point that Stepan Trofimovich assures Varvara that this was, "... merely the first stormy impulses of an overabundant constitution, that the sea would grow calm, and that it all resembled the youth of Prince Harry, carousing with Falstaff, Poins, and Mistress Quickly as described by Shakespeare." (10:36)

Overabundant constitution? Perhaps the decisive clue given to us touching upon this question can be found in Shakespeare's own account of Prince Harry's carousing. It will be recalled that at the end of Scene I, Act 2, of Henry IV, part I, Prince Harry (the future King Henry V) makes the crucial statement with regard to his own view of his youthful wild behavior:

> I know you all, and will awhile uphold
> The unyoked humour of your idleness.
> Yet herein will I imitate the sun,
> Who doth permit the base contagious clouds
> To smother up his beauty from the world,
> That when he please again to be himself,
> Being wanted he may be more wond'red at,
> By breaking through the foul and ugly mists
> Of vapours that did seem to strangle him.
> (I.ii.187-195)

Thus, by his own admission, Harry's wild behavior is only an act, designed to increase his stature in the end. His youthful wildness is not an indicator of his lack of virtue.

There is, however, an added component to this. Later in the play, in a prayer that the now King Henry V says just before the battle of Agincourt, we see the following words:

> O God of battles, steel my soldiers' hearts,
> Possess them not with fear! Take from them now
> The sense of reck'ning, or th' opposed numbers
> Pluck their hearts from them. Not today, O Lord,
> O, not today, think not upon the fault
> My father made in compassing the crown!
> I Richard's body have interred new,
> And on it have bestowed more contrite tears
> Than from it issued forced drops of blood.
> Five hundred poor I have in yearly pay,
> Who twice a day their withered hands hold up
> Toward heaven, to pardon blood;
> And I have built two chantries,
> Where the sad and solemn priests sing still

For Richard's soul. More will I do:
Though all that I can do is nothing worth;
Since that my penitence comes after all,
Imploring pardon.
(IV.i.294-310)

It thus does not require a great deal of intuition to conclude that Harry was, in point of fact, rebelling as a young man against what he perceived as the dishonorable behavior of his father. This is a view that neither Varvara Petrovna nor Stepan Trofimovich consider when they refer to Nikolai as Prince Hal. It seems quite likely that Nikolai was indeed committing a Hal-like rebellion based upon a rage he felt for his mother who had always put him at such a distance and dealt with him so coldly. As we will see, he was also testing his "moral sensuousness."

Strangely, Varvara is comforted by the Hal/Nikolai analogy. Does it not bother her that such an analogy would put her in the position of being Hal's father—a dishonorable murderer against whom Harry was rebelling? More than likely, this deeper significance never occurs to her. Her positive reaction stems from the fact that Hal's mother was royal, which by implication means that she is royal as well. As a vain woman, this is flattering.[2]

In point of fact, Varvara Petrovna's love for her son is a vain love. Indeed, we learn that Varvara, ". . . was very interested in her son's successes in Petersburg high society. Where she had not succeeded, the young officer, rich and with expectations, would succeed." (10:36) She would not only live vicariously through his successes, but bask in his reflection. This idea is one of the first we encounter in the novel as the narrator reminds us that her trip to St. Petersburg was primarily designed to renew her high connections. The visit to her son was only a "public" pretext for her own advancement. (10:21)

None of this is to argue that she does not love her son. She clearly does. After Nikolai had left town after his three scandalous attacks upon the local people, we are reminded that Varvara rarely received letters from him. While she accepted this without complaint, ". . . every day of those three years she worried about her Nicolas, missed him, and continually dreamed of him." (10:45) This is fine and good. However, Varvara's vanity interferes with her actually demonstrating this love to her son. This is the cause of Nikolai's tragedy. At the end of the day, he can never know a love not shown.

Varvara's vanity is blinding with regard to individual character. As mentioned earlier, she tries to protect her son's social standing by marrying off Dasha to Stepan, thus helping to ensure that Nikolai would marry Lizaveta. Because she sees her son as a reflection of herself, her vanity cannot allow for Nikolai to marry such a lowly girl as Dasha. She has no moral compunction to marrying off her companion of twenty years to her charge half his age in order to preserve her societal reputation (through her son). Ironically, Varvara's desire is that Nikolai marry Lizaveta, a young cosmopolitan woman of high society, who is lacking in virtue (she sleeps with Nikolai with the understanding that nothing lasting would come of it). In an age of Victorian values, Dasha clearly emerges as the higher quality woman in this regard.[3] The status-conscious, and cosmopolitan, Varvara is blind to this.

Varvara's vanity is central to her identity. Her love for her son is a vain love. This becomes crystal clear at the end of the novel, once Varvara realizes that Nikolai is linked to the various scandals occurring in town. Because her vanity compels her to consider his actions as a reflection upon her, she disavows her son by stating, "I have no son!"[4] (10:507) In other words, now that her son has become thoroughly disreputable, she no longer recognizes him as her son.

Nikolai's Cold, Calm Rage

Nikolai Vsevolodovich is deeply wounded and angry at the self-interested, vain, and incomplete love shown to him by his mother (and only parent). This results in a malicious anger in Nikolai that the narrator feels is somewhat unique. He notes that this anger is, ". . . cold, calm, and, if one may put it so, *judicious*, and therefore the most repulsive and terrible that can be." (10:165)[5]

This judiciousness leads Nikolai to carefully calculate the targets of his wrath. Because he realizes that his mother considers him a reflection upon her, he publicly engages in disgraceful behavior with the specific intent of embarrassing her. It is precisely because Varvara values her St. Petersburg high society connections that he associates with the disreputable riff-raff of the town. Because she values her connections with the Governor, Nikolai attacks him by biting his ear. Because she values the opinion of the town's elite, he grabs an elderly man's nose in the club. Most importantly, because Varvara is a woman, the most scandalous of all his behaviors are directed against women (her included). The most obvious case of this can be found in his marriage to Marya Lebyadkina.

It will be recalled that, at the first meeting of mother and son in the novel, Varvara Petrovna welcomes him after years of separation by simply sitting up straight in her chair and confronting him with questions regarding this purported marriage to this "unfortunate lame woman." (10:146) She asks him in the most formal of possible ways, "Is she your lawful wife?" (10:146)[6] His response seems calculated to inflict the greatest amount of humiliating damage. Knowing that ambiguity is particularly difficult for his mother, he simply kisses her hand without answering. He then motions gently to Marya and kindly and gently tells her that she can not be there and leads her out of the room. Through this kindness, Nikolai wants to convey his supposed love for the "lame" Marya. Because Varvara's love for her son is primarily a vain one, Nikolai's love for such a lowly, lame woman is simply humiliating for her.

Later in the novel, Nikolai Vsevolodovich finally admits in public (in front of Varvara's social rival Yulia Mikhailovna) that he is indeed married to Marya. The narrator recalls, "I will never forget the horror that was expressed on Varvara Petrovna'a face. With an insane look she rose from her chair, defending herself by holding her right hand up in front of her. Nikolai Vsevolodovich looked at her, at Liza, at the spectators, and suddenly smiled with boundless haughtiness; unhurriedly, he walked out of the room." (10:353)

Nikolai Vsevolodovich takes clear joy in publicly humiliating his mother in front of her great rival, Yulia Mikhailovna. This is, of course, uncharitable to Varvara and cruel to Marya. Deep-down in her conscience, however, Varvara does suspect that something extraordinary has contributed to the creation of this angry "beast." Varvara first indicates that she understands the deeply troubled nature of Nikolai just after his attack upon the elderly Gaganov. The narrator notes that most in the town felt that the attack was an exemplar of calculated bad behavior, not evidence of clinical madness. Varvara Petrovna thought something quite different. She immediately assumed that this was going to be the beginning of a whole string of unacceptable acts. She simply states, "It's begun!" (10:40) She was, of course, correct.

The Shamed Demon

On a purely human level, the resentment felt by Nikolai Vsevolodovich is natural under the circumstances. The source of Nikolai's emotional deadness, his nihilism, can be found in his childhood neglect. It is, however, manifest in different ways. One may quite logically surmise that all boys desire the love of their fathers. When such love is not forthcoming, many boys strive to excel in arenas that are appreciated by the father in an attempt to gain the desired love and admiration. Although he never verbalizes this, and perhaps it never actually occurs to him, this is why Pyotr Stepanovich so desires to excel within the field of radical politics. In other words, he will out-do his own father.

For Dostoevsky, the absence of maternal love seems to have much more dramatic consequences. Because the love of a mother is natural, even automatic, the lack of it produces a profound self-doubt in the child as to his "lovability." Indeed, if a mother does not love her own child, who will?

This lack of maternal love produces in Nikolai Vsevolodovich a deep-seated sense of shame and self-loathing that results in his "death of self." As mentioned above, such "self-dead" individuals may very well commit acts of violence in order to test their "self-dead" status.[7] As mentioned in chapter 1, James Gilligan found in interviews with hardened prisoners in jail that, "Many described committing the most horrific atrocities in order to see if they could feel anything, and were surprised and disappointed to see that even that did not restore a capacity to have feelings and feel alive."[8] As we will see shortly, this is precisely the path taken by Nikolai Vsevolodovich.

Nikolai is perhaps the most compelling demon in the novel. At times, he is capable of extremely despicable behavior. At other times, he behaves politely and diplomatically. In fact, in many ways, he is rather normal or commonplace. Long before Hannah Arendt popularized the concept of the "banality of evil," Dostoevsky actually presents to us a rather "banal" demon.

Physically, Nikolai is the opposite of the popularized monster of *The Exorcist*. Our narrator describes Nikolai as handsome; he is "elegant" and a gentleman of "the most refined decorum." (10:37) The narrator notes that this made him attractive to the women in town, who, "lost their minds" over him, and to the men who looked to him to "raise their banner." (10:37 & 10:201) At the same time, there was something slightly off about his physical appearance. The narrator notes that, ". . . his hair was somehow too black, his light-colored eyes were somehow too calm and clear, his complexion was somehow too soft and pale, his color somehow too bright and clean, his teeth like pearls, his lips like coral—it seemed as if he was the very image of beauty, but at the same time repulsive. People said his face resembled a mask. . . ." (10:37)

Masks, of course, are intended to hide. Was this handsome mask intended to conceal a hideous nature beneath? Dostoevsky seems to imply precisely this. It is not just his physical appearance that is deceitful, but also his behavior. With the exception of the three aforementioned attacks, which occur at the beginning of the novel, Nikolai is almost always magnanimous and courteous in public. Those around him seemed anxious to attribute his behavior to illness or delirium. We must remember, however, that Dostoevsky intends for Nikolai to be both an individual character as well as an image of an idea—nihilism. In making the image of nihilism attractive, he can easily explain how it spreads so readily. After all, something that is hideous is rejected outright by most.

There are two events in particular that highlight Nikolai's use of public magnanimity in order to make him more attractive to others. The first is seen during his duel with Gaganov, the son of the man he offends at the beginning of the book by grabbing his nose and leading him around by it. He offers apologies on many occasions, designed to show remorse and a desire for reconciliation. Once it becomes clear that a duel will be fought, Nikolai insists that if neither of the participants are injured or killed in the first round, a second and third round will be fought. The duel ends with Nikolai consistently refusing to kill Gaganov.

The effect of this behavior was quite positive among the town's people. The narrator writes, "Many of his former enemies firmly proclaimed themselves to be his friends." (10:231) He was now, ". . . in fashion." (10:234)

Yet another example of this public magnanimity occurs at the novel's revolutionary meeting. Quite in contrast with Pyotr Stepanovich's behavior, Nikolai Vsevolodovich's conduct during this meeting is magnanimous. While Pyotr arrogantly sprawls himself on a chair, Nikolai Stavrogin politely and meekly bows to all at the meeting. (10:305) While Pyotr arrogantly cuts his nails and makes a series of impetuous requests during the speeches, Nikolai quietly listens.

In spite of this magnanimity and physical attractiveness, three different characters have glimpses of the true underlying nature of Nikolai. The first is Captain Lebyadkin who, as already mentioned, describes Nikolai as a "wise serpent." (10:83) Lebyadkin, the drunken fool, actually understands Nikolai's deceptive nature, likening him to the serpent of the Garden of Eden. In essence,

Nikolai is "wise" in understanding that he must appear kind and magnanimous if he is to be attractive to others.

The second person to recognize danger in Nikolai Vsevolodovich is his lame wife, Marya Lebyadkina. In one remarkable scene, Nikolai visits Marya, to whom he was married. Dostoevsky writes about this scene, ". . . but suddenly, after almost a minute's pause, the poor woman's face took on an expression of complete horror; spasms ran across it, she raised her hands, shaking them, and suddenly began to cry, just like a frightened child; in another moment she would have screamed. But the visitor came to his senses; in an instant his expression changed, and he approached the table with a most amiable and tender smile." (10:215) As the conversation with her continues, "She wanted to say something more, but suddenly again, for the third time, the same fright instantly distorted her face, and she again recoiled, raising her hand in front of her." (10:217) Marya seems able to recognize the demonic nature of Nikolai at moments when his guard is down. In the end, she not only refuses to go to Switzerland with him but claims that he is an imposter—a pretender to the throne. (10:218-219) In other words, he only pretends to be noble; in reality he is an imposter.

As might be expected, even his own mother has concerns about Nikolai's underlying nature. The narrator writes, "And yet she was obviously afraid of him and seemed like a perfect slave before him. It was apparent that she was afraid of something indefinite, mysterious, which she herself would have been unable to explain, and oftentimes she studied Nicolas unobtrusively and attentively, pondering and puzzling over something . . . and then—the beast suddenly put out its claws." (10:38)

Yet another indicator that Varvara Petrovna suspects something far more significant than youthful bluster in Nikolai Vsevolodovich's behavior is seen in yet another point in the novel, when she walks into a room in which Nikolai is either sleeping or deep in thought. The narrator writes, "She stood over him for about three minutes, scarcely breathing, and was suddenly overcome with fear; she went out on tiptoe, paused in the doorway, hastily made a cross over him, and withdrew unnoticed, with a new heavy feeling, and a new anguish." (10:182) It is interesting to think of this proud, vain and cosmopolitan woman resorting to humble Christian prayer. Just as with Stepan Trofimovich, in moments of crisis, religion serves as a point of comfort.[9]

This is important. For Dostoevsky, religion represents the opposite of nihilism. When either Stepan Trofimovich or Varvara Petrovna encounters nihilism in its purest form, they resort back to religion—the counterforce to nihilism.

Nikolai's Ever Escalating Nihilistic Journey

Aside from the two Lebyadkins, the townspeople of Skvoreshniki remain remarkably in the dark about Nikolai's nihilistic nature, even after, ". . . the beast suddenly showed its claws." (10:38) Aside from his attempts to mask these behaviors, we see an escalation of harm done to others as he increasingly pushes the moral limit of his nihilism. As already mentioned, he begins his nihilistic journey with three "insolent" acts (10:38) The first attack finds its source in a habitual phrase uttered by the elderly Pavel Pavlovich Gaganov—"No, sir, they won't lead me by the nose!" (10:38) Nikolai seems to have taken notice of this oft-repeated expression and decided to use it as the basis for his humiliation. Nikolai grabs the elderly man by the nose, and literally leads him around the room. The narrator notes, ". . . at the very moment of the operation he was almost in a trance, 'as if he had lost his mind' . . . [he] smiled gaily and maliciously, 'without the least repentance." (10:39) As his attacks become more insolent, he finds it more and more difficult to recognize the harm in them.

The second insolent act seems, at least by modern standards, somewhat innocuous as well. Nikolai's victim in this case is Madame Liputin, the wife of the one Fourierist in the terrorist cell. She is described as a very pretty little lady, who is terribly shy of Nikolai Vsevolodovich. At a party, during which Nikolai dances twice with her and amicably chats with her, he suddenly puts his arm around her waist and kisses her three times on the lips in front of everyone at the party. Madame Liputin feints as a result. (10:41)

This is followed by the third "insolent" act, in which Nikolai attacks the Governor, Ivan Ossipovich. The Governor had called Nikolai to see him in order to question him about the preceding two attacks. When asked what had prompted him to commit these acts, Nikolai responds by biting the governor's ear. The enraged Governor throws him in jail.

Once the "scientific" basis for these attacks is determined—"brain fever"—he is released from jail. The following Spring he begins a three-year trip through Europe and the Near East. During this long tour we learn that he seduces Darya, and Marya Shatova (whom he impregnates) and courts Lizaveta. Today such behavior might be winked at, referred to as "caddish." Having such sexual experience in a premarital context in nineteenth century Russia, however, rendered a woman "disreputable" and destroyed any chances of future marriage.

As we learn, Nikolai's behavior becomes increasingly insolent throughout the book. We learn that he marries Lebyadkin's sister (also named Marya) after a drunken dinner in order to test the limits of his nihilism. (10:211) Shatov understands this and explains to Nikolai that he married her, "Precisely because here the disgrace and senselessness arrived at the point of genius! . . . You married out of a passion for torture, out of a passion for remorse, out of moral sensuality. It was from nervous strain. . . . The challenge to common sense was too enticing!" (10:202) In essence, he marries Marya in order to experience and feel moral baseness. After all, what could be more base than marrying a mentally and physically retarded woman on a bet?[10]

Nikolai descends to the very depths of moral baseness with the seduction and tragic death of the young daughter of his landlady, Matryosha.[11] As we find in the chapter "At Tikhon's," a chapter initially deemed too offensive to include with the publication of the rest of the novel, Nikolai decides to seduce the harshly treated fourteen-year-old daughter of his landlady.[12] He does this in order to further test his "moral sensuality." After the seduction, he rejects her and refuses to sooth or comfort her in her anxiety as she is concerned that she had "killed God." Several days later, she commits suicide over this in the outhouse. Importantly, he does not try to intervene in the suicide as he hears her prepare for and commit this final act. He simply sits quietly and listens. After it is over, he admits to feeling something about this, but is unsure what exactly it is. He asks, "Is this what is called remorse of conscience or repentance?" (11:22)

Some time after this incident, Nikolai travels to the Savior-St. Yefimi-Bogorodsky monastery, on the outskirts of town with the intention of meeting with a retired Bishop Tikhon. The narrator writes that, "Nikolai Vsevolodovich was still in a state of great distraction caused by some inner anxiety that was oppressing him." (11:7) He spoke with unaccustomed sincerity, "that it seemed the former man, suddenly and inadvertently, had vanished in him completely. He was not even slightly ashamed to show the fear with which he spoke about his phantom." (11:9)

What is this phantom? Importantly, it is not the phantom of conscience. It is the phantom of self-death. Nikolai seduced this young girl in order to test his moral sensuousness. Would he feel remorse for having done this act? After her suicide, and his consequent lack of remorse, he became aware that he should feel something, but does not. He writes, "And generally I was bored with life then, to the point of stupefaction. Once the danger was past, I completely forgot about the incident. . . ." (11:20) This provokes the trip to see Bishop Tikhon.

In his confession to Tikhon, Stavrogin writes, "Every extremely shameful, endlessly humiliating, mean, and, above all, ridiculous position I have happened to get into in my life has always aroused in me, along with boundless wrath, and unbelievable pleasure." (11:14) As Tikhon realizes, it is not pleasure at all that Stavrogin experiences. Tikhon knows that Stavrogin has written for effect, in order to make the reader hate him all the more. Tikhon explains, ". . . their hatred will evoke yours, and, hating, it will be easier for you than if you were to accept their pity?" (11:25)

Just as Stavrogin can not feel remorse, he can not feel pleasure. His soul, the seat of all human sentiments, is dead. No disgraceful act, no murder, no infamy could provoke this soul to feel any sort of remorse.

The Nihilistic Contagion

The escalation of Nikolai's nihilism is also seen in other people throughout the town. It is almost as if the nihilism introduced by Nikolai Vsevolodovich is a disease, spreading from one person to the next. As the town prepares for the crowning fete, we see this in one quite remarkable series of events.

In the chapter entitled "Before the Fete," the narrator recalls a most unusual day trip led by Lizaveta Nikolaevna. The goal of the outing is to visit the "holy fool" Semyon Yakovlevich who had been living in the home of a rich merchant just across the river from town. The number of individuals participating in the journey is large, including both Nikolai as well as Pyotr.

Just as they pass the town's hotel, they hear that a suicide had just occurred there. Out of a desire for pure entertainment, they hurry in to see that a young nineteen-year-old man, who had spent his family's hard-earned rubles by carousing in town, had just shot himself. The 400 rubles that he had flitted away was all the money that the family had. It was to be used for his sister's wedding. Upon encountering this scene, the members of Lizaveta's traveling party are thrilled. They were looking for entertainment and the young man's suicide seemed as good as anything else for this purpose. They greedily and merrily examine the body, the table on which his last dinner is still to be found, and everything else associated with the suicide. In fact, at one point, Lyamshin actually grabs a small bunch of grapes from the dead man's table. Another, laughingly, follows his example. Once the police chief arrives, the group of on-lookers is asked to leave. The narrator writes that for the remaining portion of the trip, ". . . the general happiness, laughter, and brisk chatter became almost twice as lively." (10:256)

Perhaps the most extreme example of the degree to which this nihilism can spread is found in the story describing their actual visit to Semyon Yakovlevich. As the outing party arrive, they see that there are dozens of visitors already there. These visitors are seeking blessings from the "holy fool." We quickly learn that his behavior is erratic, at best. In fact, his behavior is the opposite of what you would expect from a venerated man. In handing out tea, he bypasses the poor and has a cup poured for a rich merchant. He then insists that four helpings of sugar be placed in it. A woman who seeks advice about how to deal with her children is given three sugarloaves and kicked out of the room in an abusive manner. When the landlord himself asks for help in controlling his quick temper, he is also kicked out of the room with abuse. The gold coin he left is given to the rich merchant. Lastly, upon the third request from one lady of the outing to utter something of significance, he turns to her and said, "F. . . you, F. . . you." (10:260) In reaction to this, the horrified women hurry out of the room while the men burst into "Homeric" laughter.

What is the meaning of all this? Clearly, Dostoevsky is presenting us with this to convey the message that nihilism spreads to all sectors of society. Literally no one is immune—not even the Church. Lizaveta and her party are clearly behaving in a nihilistic manner by taking pleasure in the sight of a dead nineteen-year-old and in the outrageous behavior of a "holy fool." The question therefore becomes, if Lizaveta herself has been infected, what is its source?

Dostoevsky gives us a clue to this at the end of this passage, when, as she is escorting the recently humiliated Mavriky Nikolaevich out of the house, she runs into Nikolai Vsevolodovich. The narrator writes, "It was asserted, on the contrary, and quite seriously, that Liza, having looked at Nikolai Vsevolodovich, quickly raised her hand, right up to the level of his face, and would certainly have struck him if he had not managed to draw back." (10:261) Timing here is important. She saw him in a moment of guilt for having humiliated Mavriky. In reacting in such a way, she was acknowledging Nikolai is the source of her descent into nihilism.

Indeed, Lizaveta is not a nihilist throughout most of the novel. The narrator describes her as a vain, cosmopolitan, high-society woman who was educated by Stepan Trofimovich. Breaking with usual tradition, she rides horses in public, appearing, "as a conqueror, and to conquer" (10:89) Like Varvara, she desires to dominate—particularly men close to her. At one point, she introduces Stepan Trofimovich, to her fiancé Mavriky Nikolaevich, by saying, "He is the best and most faithful man on the whole earth, and you must come to love him as you do me! *He does everything I want* [in French]." (10:87)[13]

Like Stepan Trofimovich she has certain cosmopolitan intellectual tendencies. The narrator tells of her approaching Shatov with the idea of publishing a yearbook of all events that occurred throughout the year. This yearbook would be, ". . . limited only to events that more or less expressed the personal moral life of the people, the personality of the Russian people at a given moment." (10:103) Much like Stepan's interests, there is really nothing involved with this project of any significant content—no depth, no originality.

It is not until Nikolai Vsevolodovich appears in town that she begins her journey from vain, high-society women to a nihilist. As we already know, Nikolai pursued her in Switzerland, but it is not until the end of the novel that we know that he succeeds in seducing her (in Skvoreshniki). This represents her ultimate defeat to nihilism. As a nihilist, she loses her ability to care about others. The morning after her seduction, Nikolai asks her, "You won't abandon me . . . we'll leave together, this very day, right? Right?" (10:399) Once he hears her negative responses, he asks her, "Liza! What was it yesterday, then?" Her nihilistic response of, "It was what it was," leads to a crack in Nikolai's nihilistic armor. He responds, "That's impossible! That's cruel." (10:399)

By the very end of the novel Nikolai Vsevolodovich seems to have come to the conclusion that he is indeed "self-dead," and that nothing can be done about it. Like Stepan Trofimovich, he decides upon an escape to nature. Rather than a quest to the Russian countryside, he opts for an escape to Switzerland. Nikolai tells us about this in his last letter to Darya. He writes, "Last year, like Herzen, I registered as a citizen of canton Uri, and no one knows it." (10:513) He informs her that he had already bought a little house there. He adds, "It's a very dull place, a narrow valley, the mountains restrict both vision and thought. . . . I am not well, but I hope to get rid of hallucinations in that air." (10:513) He then states, "I expect nothing of Uri; I am simply going. I have not chosen a gloomy place on purpose. I have no ties in Russia—everything is as alien to me there as everywhere. It's true that I dislike living there more than anywhere; but I can't hate anything even there!" (10:513-514) Nikolai Vsevolodovich senses that the nature of the Swiss mountains *should be* beautiful, but he can not appreciate it.

On one level, Nikolai chooses Uri because he feels no connection to his homeland. He is a stateless person, just like Herzen. However, it is far more significant that he describes Switzerland as "gloomy." He mentions this twice. How could the clean, crisp, alpine, bright air of Uri ever be described as "gloomy"? There is only one answer. He is unable to appreciate the beauty of the place. He does not know or understand beauty because he has no ideals. It is all the same to him. His dead soul is not receptive to beauty. This disappoints him.

It is not just Nikolai that reacts this way. This is very similar to *The Idiot*'s Prince Myshkin, who is also not cured by the mountain air. He remains an "idiot" even after returning to Switzerland. A rejection of cosmopolitan culture, and an escape from the city are not enough. For Dostoevsky, the disease of cosmopolitanism can only be cured by embracing the ideals that it rejects. This is done by embracing the Gods of the Jews, Greeks, and Romans. For Dostoevsky, what is required is a spiritual and moral redemption, not a physical one.

The Creation of New Cosmopolitan Gods

Nikolai Vsevolodovich is aware of his self-dead status and is unhappy with it. He also wants to know where it will lead him. In order to examine this, Nikolai attempts to convert Shatov and Kirillov to atheism in order to understand two possible reactions to life without God.[14] To state it slightly differently, they are meant to illustrate the most extreme form of rootless cosmopolitanism—atheism.

In keeping with Dostoevsky's understanding of Tocqueville, it should not surprise us that both of these rootless intellectuals journey to America in order to test out their newly adopted rootless condition. They took laborer jobs, were exploited, and fired. For four months, the two of them lay destitute in a small house with no plans and no ideas. Eventually, Shatov (ostensibly so does Kirillov) receives 100 rubles from Stavrogin and they both return to Europe. Upon arriving back in Switzerland, Shatov announces that he intends to break with the revolutionary radicals. This eventually becomes the pretext for his murder. Kirillov does not break with them, but agrees to allow his suicide to cover for Shatov's murder.

It is no coincidence that before the pair had left for America in the novel, Stavrogin had tested his atheistic theories out on each one of them. Because he was so conflicted about this question, he planted this atheistic seed in each of them so as to see how these theories would play out in their minds. He then carefully observes them.

Nikolai Vsevolodovich takes a particular interest in Kirillov, an atheist who believes that there is no idea higher than that there is no God. He has come to the highly unusual conclusion that since God is necessary, but does not exist, he must shoot himself to demonstrate this paradox. He explains, "If there is God, then the will is all his, and I can not free myself from his will. But if the will is all mine, it is my duty to proclaim self-will." (10:470) By killing himself he will be proclaiming not only that God is dead, but that he is expressing a god-like self-will by shooting himself. He explains,

> . . . I will proclaim self-will, it is my duty to believe that I do not believe. I will begin and end, and open the door. And save. Only this one thing will save all

> men and in the next generation transform them physically; for in the present physical aspect, so far as I have thought, it is not possible for man to be without the former God. For three years I have been searching for the attribute of my god-like status, and I have found it: the attribute of my god-like status is—self-will. (11:472)

It is in this way that Kirillov becomes God.[15]

Kirillov's eventual suicide is but a precursor to Nikolai Vsevolodovich's. Both characters seem to know this. Nikolai seeks out Kirillov to delve into his motivations because he himself has contemplated suicide. Kirillov understands Nikolai's motivations in observing him. He explains Nikolai's confusion by stating, ". . . if Stavrogin believes, he does not believe that he believes. If he does not believe, he does not believe that he does not believe." (10:469)

Shatov, on the other hand, is an atheist who does not deify himself, but his nation. He begins his argument with the assertion that great nations are created by a moral force—a force largely characterized by a "seeking for God." For Shatov, the Jews, the Ancient Greeks and the Romans are three "great" nations because they had their own Gods. Once the particularism of a nation's God disappears, so does its greatness.

Shatov, then takes one more step down this line of logic by arguing that it is not so much that nations have their unique Gods, but that the nation itself becomes God. He explains, "The goal of all the activities of nations, of every nation and in every period of its existence, is solely the seeking for God, its own God, entirely its own, and faith in him as the only true one. God is the synthetic person of the whole nation. . . ." (10:198) For Shatov, the nation becomes God—or in his words, ". . . I raise the nation up to God." (10:199)

Shatov, however, is conflicted about this approach. On the one hand, he believes in the importance of believing in a divine God. On the other, he simply cannot do it himself. Notably, when Stavrogin asks Shatov if he believes in God, the best he can answer is, "I . . . I will believe in God." (10:201)

Ultimately, Shatov believes that Stavrogin is the end result of the death of the Gods. Implicit in his understanding is the fact that it is caused by cosmopolitanism. After all, cosmopolitan culture argues against specific ideals and virtues. Cosmopolitans reject absolute ideals. There are no great or small nations. All are equal and all are of equal worth. The Gods have lost their distinctiveness—and value.

God's Love, Vanity, and Demonic Nihilism

It is no coincidence that Nikolai Vsevolodovich's story ends with suicide. This physical "self-death" parallels the psychological "self-death" already experienced as a neglected child. Dostoevsky clearly wanted to illustrate what he felt was the psychological toll of cosmopolitanism, an ideology that replaces the ancient Gods with modern ones. To state it another way, for Dostoevsky, if you replace God's love with cosmopolitan vanity, self-death will result. This self-death will result in all sorts of evils. To state it differently, cosmopolitanism produces demons.

Just as Stepan Trofimovich admits toward the end of his life that he is a leading demon, so does Nikolai Vsevolodovich. Nikolai states this when he responds to Darya's sentence, "May God preserve you from your dark spirit, and . . . call me, call me soon!" He responds, "Oh, he's no dark spirit! He's simply a nasty, disease-ridden little demon with a runny nose, a failure." (10:231)

In the end, Christian belief holds that a return to God's law of faith, hope, and love provide for the liberation from demonic possession. This is precisely the point of the once-banned chapter, "At Tikhon's." Nikolai goes to Bishop Tikhon to ask for repentance, perhaps recognizing that this was the way out of his moral abyss. In the end, just as Stepan Trofimovich seems unable to pull off a convincing and genuine conversion to faith, hope, and charity, so Nikolai is unable to do it as well.

The Biblical serpent is the cursed animal because he so cleverly convinces humanity to eat the forbidden fruit from the tree of knowledge. Mankind is promised God-like status if he should eat from the tree. The fruit from the tree of nihilism seems equally as enticing. It does not promise knowledge, but freedom from conscience. In many ways, this can seem attractive to individuals who grapple with moral dilemmas on a daily basis. It is attractive to terrorists for precisely the same reason. Just as in the Garden of Eden, there is a price to pay for eating from the tree. This is the topic of our next chapter, the paradox of nihilistic terrorism.

Notes

1. It should be recalled that Pyotr Stepanovich was raised by his aunts in a remote province six hundred miles from Skvoreshniki. It seems quite logical to assume, therefore, that Pyotr Stepanovich was not exposed to the same degree of neglect as was Nikolai Vsevolodovich.

2. Robert Belknap wrote insightfully about the role of Hamlet in this novel. See Robert Belknap, "Shakespeare and the Possessed," *Dostoevsky Studies*, Volume 5, 1984 (http://www.utoronto.ca/tsq/DS/05/063.shtml, 7 March 2007).

3. Dasha is also seduced by Nikolai in Switzerland, however she never alludes to this experience by referring to it, as Lizaveta does, as a meaningless act.

4. Of course, by this point, she actually did not have a son.

5. The word "judicious" (*razumniy*) here is usually translated as "reasonable." In my reading of this, the meaning centers upon the fact that he carefully calculates the targets and effects of his attacks.

6. The use of the Russian formal pronoun "vy" between mother and son is most unnatural.

7. James Gilligan, "Shame, Guilt, and Violence," *Social Research* 70, No. 4 (Winter 2003): 1149-1181.

8. James Gilligan, "Shame, Guilt, and Violence," 1152.

9. There are other signs of her, at least partial, adherence to Christian practice. She seems to attend church services, at least occasionally. This is where she meets Marya

Timofeevna Lebyadkina for the first time. Varvara also has a "big bronze crucifix in the corner" in her drawing room. (10:127)

10. We must be careful, however, in assuming that Nikolai married Marya only out of a desire to punish himself. When Shatov accuses him of marrying Marya for this reason, Stavrogin responds by saying, "You're a psychologist . . . though you are partially mistaken about the reasons for my marriage." (10:202) Yes, self-torture was a part of it, but he also seems to genuinely desire love—the point at the very root of his problems. At the end of his conversation with Shatov, in a very non-nihilistic sort of way, Nikolai asks him to watch out for Marya "just in case." (10:203) In an earlier conversation with Kirillov, Nikolai states about Marya, "You assume, Mr. Kirillov, that I am laughing at her; let me assure you that I do indeed respect her, because she is better than any of us." (10:150)

11. It is perhaps worth noting that the most extreme violations against women committed by Nikolai are against women named after "Mary." The married Marya Shatova is impregnated by him, the lame Marya Lebyadkina is wed to him, and the adolescent Matryosha is seduced by him (and then commits suicide). His other female conquests in the novel, Lizaveta and Darya, are mere one-time seductions.

12. In one place she is referred to as being fourteen years old (11:13), in another place, ten years old. (11:22)

13. The irony of her saying this in French should not be lost on the reader.

14. Many have assumed that Shatov's opinions are identical with those of Dostoevsky. This is quite unlikely—Shatov is an atheist. Dostoevsky created Shatov and Kirillov in order to contrast two possible reactions to life without God. This is quite similar to Dostoevsky's depiction of Myshkin and Rogozhin in *The Idiot*. In *The Idiot*, he does not validate either the pure *agape* of Myshkin, nor the pure *eros* of Rogozhin.

15. In an earlier conversation with Stavrogin, Kirillov uses the term *chelovokobog* ("man-God"). (10:189)

Chapter 5
The Paradox of Nihilistic Terrorism

In *The Demons*, Dostoevsky not only demonstrates the *source* of nihilism and terrorism in nineteenth century Russia, but how terrorist managers compel their followers to kill innocent people in the name of a political idea. He illustrates this through the activities of Pyotr Stepanovich Verkhovensky, and, in so doing, provides a psychological approach to terrorist management that applies to a wide spectrum of psychological types.

In order to illustrate this in the clearest of possible ways, Dostoevsky has Pyotr Stepanovich lead a notional terrorist cell consisting of five radically differing individuals. Shigalyov has created an ideology of his own (which argues for totalitarian terror), while Liputin follows the ideas of Charles Fourier. Virginsky seems to be committed only to a deep feeling of sentimentalism. The remaining two terrorists, Lyamshin and Tolkatchenko, have no other ideology but roguishness.

How is a terrorist manager to lead such a motley crew? At one point in the novel, Stavrogin suggests to Pyotr Stepanovich that he should cement the group together by involving them all in a murder (of Shatov). In the end, even this strategy fails as a terrorist management device. Is this to suggest that Dostoevsky believed that no effective technique could be used to manage such a cell? Yes and no. As he does with other such themes within the book, Dostoevsky provides for the reader a clue in answering this question through a passing reference to a commonly read work of the day. In this case, it is to Shakespeare's *Hamlet*.

Hamlet and Human Conscience

It will be recalled that in the chapter entitled, "The Wise Serpent," Peter Stepanovich, in an effort to console Varvara Petrovna about her son's purported marriage to Marya Lebyadkina (the lame sister of the drunkard Lebyadkin), assures her that it is not Shakespeare's Hal that Nikolai resembles, but Hamlet. He explains that Nikolai Vsevolodovich was not motivated by base emotions, but by some higher calling in marrying the lame girl. Relieved by this analogy, Varvara states: "But Nicolas had neither a Horatio, nor an Ophelia. He had only his mother, but what can a mother do alone and in such circumstances?" (10:151)

This is indeed the question with which Hamlet's mother, Gertrude, is faced in Shakespeare's great tragedy. Should she, as a royal widow, retire into the background and allow her son to take the throne? Or should she leap into an "o'er-hasty" and adulterous marriage in pursuit of satiating her lustful passion and in doing so, keeping her son from inheriting the crown.[1] Gertrude, of course, chooses that latter course. In so doing, numerous tragic deaths occur (including her own).

This is, of course, not the main theme of Hamlet. Hamlet's main theme revolves around Hamlet himself, and the dilemma he faces (whether to kill the king usurper or not). Because Varvara Petrovna is so terribly self-absorbed, she is unable to understand perspectives that are not at least similar to her own. Even when she attempts to understand others, she is blinded by her own values and experiences. As with the previously mentioned analogy in which Nikolai is compared with Hal, Varvara is pleased with this Nikolai/Hamlet parallel. After all, if Nikolai is Hamlet, she is a queen. This is quite flattering to her vanity.

It is far more profitable, however, to understand Nikolai Vsevolodovich through this new lens. Is he truly similar to Hamlet? Is he, like Hamlet, a man of conscience? Is Pyotr Stepanovich truly correct in saying that Nikolai is guided by his conscience?

As will be seen below, in spite of his comment, Pyotr Stepanovich is attracted to Nikolai Vsevolodovich for his seeming *lack* of conscience. In Pyotr's eyes, he is quite the opposite of Hamlet. Although Pyotr is extremely insightful about human motivations and an adroit psychological manipulator of human actions, he feels that Nikolai's perceived lack of conscience is the ultimate key to successful terrorist management.

As will be seen below, Pyotr Stepanovich cleverly manipulates those around him. He quickly understands what motivates individuals and uses this knowledge to manage his terrorist cell. At the same time he recognizes that these motivations might not be enough to overcome the weight of conscience that comes with the murder of innocent individuals.

In short, Dostoevsky understands the importance of human conscience and the role that it plays in terrorism. Because most human beings are fundamentally conscience-bearing beings, the aversion to killing must be overcome for the individual terrorist. In order to illustrate this, Dostoevsky creates the character of Nikolai Vsevolodovich Stavrogin who is meant to be the "pure" nihilist—the man who has no beliefs, no values, and—therefore—no conscience. For Pyotr Stepanovich, Nikolai Vsevolodovich is the ultimate killing machine because he is free from the constraints of traditional morality *and* conscience.

With this freedom from morality and conscience comes a striking paradox. Nihilism provides the ideal moral condition for a terrorist insofar as it allows terrorists to kill without remorse. If, however, we keep in mind that terrorism is killing in the name of an idea, nihilism seems a less useful position. By banishing human conscience nihilism eliminates ideals of any kind. Without ideals, an individual cannot strive for a more perfect political world. A nihilist, after all, has no vision of "good" or "bad." Thus, on a purely theoretical level, one is left with two possible options: a remorseless terrorist without a cause or a remorseful terrorist with a cause. In the first case one is unlikely to have any terroristic activity, in the second case, only short-term terroristic activity. For a terroristic mastermind, neither situation is ideal. This is the paradox of nihilistic terrorism.

The Repulsive Serpent

We have already illustrated that Pyotr Stepanovich is motivated to commit terrorism out of a desire to acquire personal power. He claims to act in the name of a cause, but he is only out for his own personal power. Pyotr is a fraud; a "swindler" not a "socialist." (10:324)

Throughout the novel, a certain aura of foulness clings to him. Although Dostoevsky describes a glib, self-confident man who is never at a loss for the appropriate words and phrases, he also writes,

> His thoughts are calm, in spite of his hurried look, distinct and final—which is especially noticeable. His enunciation is remarkably clear; his words spill out like enormous uniform grains, always choice and always ready to be at your service. You like it at first, but later it becomes repulsive, and precisely because of this all too clear enunciation, this string of ever ready words. (10:143)

In a word, he is simultaneously repulsive and banal.

His serpent-like physical appearance matches the repulsiveness of his words. He is described as having an elongated head and a sharp face. (10:143) He then writes about his tongue, "You somehow begin to imagine that the tongue in his mouth must be of some unique shape, somehow unusually long and thin, terribly red, and with an extremely sharp, constantly and involuntarily wriggling tip." (10:144)

Pyotr Stepanovich understands that he appears repulsive to others and that this is a liability in leading others to commit terrorist acts. He admits this when he describes himself as, ". . . not stupid, not smart, rather giftless, and dropped from the moon." (10:175) He also recognizes that he lacks an ideology with which to unite his group. Although almost constant reference is made throughout the novel to the "common cause," in reality, none of the five cell members actually have anything in common ideologically.

The fact that Pyotr Stepanovich can neither motivate his terrorist cell by means of his own good leadership, nor by means of a common ideology, means that he must manage them through psychological ploys. This becomes clear at one point when he describes his techniques to Nikolai Vsevolodovich:

> I will make you laugh: what first of all works terribly well—a uniform. There's nothing stronger than a uniform. I purposely invent ranks and positions: I have secretaries, secret spies, treasurers, chairmen, registrars, their colleagues—it's all very much liked and has been completely accepted. Then the next force, it stands to reason, is sentimentality. You know, with us socialism spreads mostly through sentimentality. . . . Well, and finally the main force—the cement that bonds it all—is shame at one's own opinion. There is a real force! . . . I can get them to go through fire, if I just yell at them that they are not liberal enough. (10:298-299)

These three fundamental techniques provide the basis for his psychological ploys. At times he uses them singularly on each individual terrorist, at other times, simultaneously. Each terrorist seems to have a particular psychological need that is exploited by one of these "forces." As will be seen, all but one of these ploys is, in the end, inadequate in effectively overcoming the obstacle of the human conscience. By carefully indicating which ploy is most effective, Dostoevsky is telling us a great deal about the psychological makeup of the most dangerous type of terrorist.

Nothing Stronger Than a Uniform

While none of his terrorists are singular in terms of their psychological motivation, Pyotr Stepanovich argues that certain types of individuals can be strongly drawn to "the uniform." This force is motivating for one primary reason. By inventing "ranks and positions," a clearly discernable hierarchy is created into which each revolutionary can fit. This, in turn, provides a psychological sense of belonging for members within it. To state it another way, it also provides for each member a venue within which he can be appreciated and loved by others. If one accepts the basic principal that all human beings have the psychological need to be loved, this can provide a powerful force.

The cell member that seems most associated with this ploy is Shigalyov. We know little about him other than he is the morose man with the long ears.[2] Shigalyov advocates a theory that starts with unlimited freedom and arrives at unlimited despotism. In order to do so, he advocates the division of mankind into two unequal parts. One-tenth exercises complete and absolute freedom and unlimited power over the remaining nine-tenths. This latter group enthusiastically embrace their slave-like existence, attaining "primeval innocence, something like the Garden of Eden." (10:312)

Pyotr Stepanovich is willing to use this force to attract members to his cell. He informs the cell members that the revolutionary organization is scattered all over Russia and the world and is run from a central headquarters in Europe. In so doing, he is not only creating an elaborate hierarchy, but he is creating a sense of grandeur.

In spite of the power of this hierarchy and grandeur, this force seems to be the least powerful of Pyotr Stepanovich's three forces. The first evidence of this occurs as the terrorist cell begins to question the plan to kill Shatov. It is no coincidence that it is Shigalyov who initially encourages the others to insist that Pyotr Stepanovich should "explain himself." (10:303) On the evening of the murder itself he announces,

> Having thought through the matter, I have decided that the projected murder is not merely a waste of precious time which might be employed in a more suitable and appropriate manner, but presents, moreover, that deplorable deviation from the normal method which has always been most damaging to the cause and has delayed its triumph for scores of years, under the guidance of shallow thinkers and politically privileged men instead of purely socialistic leanings. (10:459)

He believes that the planned murder to be in contradiction to his program and walks away. Dostoevsky implies by all of this that the force of hierarchy and rank is simply not sufficiently compelling in order to motivate a terrorist recruit to commit the murder of an innocent person—a prerequisite for terrorism.

There is, however, one other plot participant who is motivated by the force of the uniform—Ensign Erkel. Not coincidently, he is the only terrorist who is actually a military man. He is, literally, a man "of the uniform."

Erkel longs to be submissive. The narrator writes that he is a "shallow" and "unreflecting character," who eternally longs to, ". . . submit to another's will . . ." (10:439) Throughout the last half of the novel, he is a quiet, loyal, and obedient member of the group. Indeed, he not only clearly and obediently cooperates in the murder of Shatov, but even once he learns that there is no vast international network of terrorists, he continues to be loyal to Pyotr Stepanovich. This is, of course, quite different than the reaction of Shigalyov, who refuses to participate at all.

Why is the force of hierarchy sufficient for Erkel to participate in the murder and not Shigalyov? The answer here seems to lie with Dostoevsky's belief that this is a psychological strategy that works most effectively on young, impressionable, and immature men like Erkel. The fact the Erkel is young and helpless is highlighted in the following description,

> Yet even the strictest of the judges trying him has been moved to some compassion—by his youth, by his helplessness, by the unmistakable evidence that he is nothing but a fanatical victim of a political impostor; and, most of all, by his conduct to his mother, to whom, as it appears, he used to send almost the half of his small salary. . . .Whatever may happen, many among us feel sorry for Erkel. (10:512)

Be this as it may, it should be mentioned that Erkel had feelings of remorse for participating in the murder of Shatov. While his dedication to Pyotr Stepanovich was sufficiently strong so as to commit the crime itself, it was not strong enough to overcome his conscience in the long run. Dostoevsky writes that after the murder, "Something else was beginning to scratch at his poor little heart, something he himself did not yet understand, something connected with the previous evening." (10:479) In fact, ". . . he spent the whole of the next day lying in bed, apparently quietly, his face turned to the wall, and without saying a word. . . ." (10:509) In spite of the power of this force, his conscience burdened him.

The Force of Sentimentality

Sentimentality is, in essence, an exaggerated insistence upon the importance of emotional sentiments, in opposition to reason. A sentimentalist experiences and displays an intense feeling of love which is focused upon an ideal condition or concept. If the "force of the uniform" provides a formal structure within which members can feel belonging and love, the "force of sentimentality" allows for a much more flexible and intellectualized venue to exhibit love—and ultimately to be loved by the world. Pyotr Stepanovich cleverly sees it as a force to be used to motivate certain types of cell members. The terrorist who seems most prone to sentimentality is Virginsky.

The most obvious clue to this sentimentality is that Dostoevsky overtly describes Virginsky as an "*obshchechelovek.*" (10:177) There is no exact translation in English of this word; the word in Russian is also ambiguous (and rarely used). The word "*obshche,*" the root of this word, is linked to the concept of common or general. *Obshchee soglasie* is usually translated as the "common consent;" *obshchee blago* as the "common good." An *obshechelovek* is a man who is concerned with things that are shared in common. To state it another way, he is a man concerned with the common good.[3]

Although the details of his political ideology are never laid out, Virginsky is ultimately committed to a purely sentimental "higher cause." No specifics are given, he is simply a "socially concerned man." The narrator backs up this interpretation by writing, "Virginsky himself was a man of rare pure heartedness, and I have seldom met more honest fervor." (10:28) At another point, the narrator recalls him saying with "shining eyes," "I will never, never, abandon these bright hopes." (10:28) The narrator continues, "Of these 'bright hopes' he always spoke quietly, in a sweet half-whisper, as if secretly." (10:28-29) No other details are provided; for Dostoevsky it does not matter—he is simply a man of pure sentiment.

As proof of the power of his sentimentality, Dostoevsky portrays him as the unconditionally loving husband. We learn that he is a quiet, self-taught, thoughtful clerk in government service. He is married to a midwife, a profession that occupies the lowest rung of the social ladder, "lower even than the priest's wife in spite of her husband's rank as an officer." (10:300) We also learn that he patiently endures his wife's sister who terrifies him "in domestic life." (10:301)

More remarkable, he tolerates an open affair that she has with the drunkard, Lebyadkin. Upon learning of the affair, Virginsky wept violently, but did not break off with her. The only retaliation we learn of involves a single physical assault upon Lebyadkin. Afterward, he pleads with his wife for forgiveness. The narrator tells us, "But this forgiveness was not granted, as he refused to apologize to Lebyadkin; furthermore, he was upbraided for the meanness of his ideas and his stupidity, the latter charge based on the fact that he knelt down to his wife while explaining all of this." (10:29)

Virginsky is clearly a sentimental man, maintaining an exaggerated insistence upon the importance of emotional sentiments, even in the face of overwhelming reason and humiliation. He also remains sentimentally attached to the idea of a "higher cause" even when he has doubts about the idea of killing Shatov. The day before the attack, Virginsky tries to stop it. The narrator recalls, "Virginsky, in the course of that day, had spent two hours in running to see the members of *our* group to inform them that Shatov would certainly not report on them, because his wife had come back and given birth to a child, and no one 'who knew anything of human nature' could suppose that Shatov could be a danger at this moment." (10:455) As a sentimental man, Virginsky is not only concerned about killing Shatov, but of harming the newly born child by killing its father.

Virginsky does not stop in his attempt to save Shatov's life, even as they are gathered together in the park just before the murder. Although he is overruled, he does not leave (as does Shigalyov). He does not, however, actively participate in the murder either. Dostoevsky writes, "Virginsky, though he had rushed to Shatov when everyone else did, had not seized him or helped to hold him." (10:461) Then, as the corpse is being prepared to be thrown into the pond, he starts to shake, and cries out, "This is not it, this is not it! No, this is not it at all!" (10:461)

Clearly the force of sentiment is stronger than the force of rank/hierarchy. Virginsky is indirectly complicit in the murder and present during its execution. Ultimately, however, he was unable to participate in the grisly task itself. Furthermore, his "common good" cause is not strong enough to act without feelings of immediate remorse. His sense of guilt is only relieved once he is arrested. Only at this point does he confess that, "a weight fell from my heart." (10:511) Overall, these actions seem to roughly correlate with the level given to the force of sentimentality by Pyotr Stepanovich. This would lead one to believe that the force of shame, his third force, is even more effective in overcoming the burden of human conscience.

The Main Force: The Force of Shame

Shame, an emotion arising from the fear of being perceived as dishonored or ridiculous, is perhaps one of the most powerful, yet underrated, of all human emotions. Just as with the "force of the uniform" and the "force of sentimentality," the "force of shame" revolves around the human need for love. To be dishonored or ridiculed is to be not loved. Just as love is a basic human need, so its opposite is to be avoided. It is for this reason that the "force of shame" is a powerful one for Dostoevsky.

Indeed, Pyotr Stepanovich argues (in the aforementioned quote) that the force of shame is one of the most powerful of motivating forces. As we saw in chapter 3, it is a force that acts on Pyotr Stepanovich himself. He is shamed by his childhood abandonment and lack of love. This results in a lack of self-love that propels him to lash out against the world. Ultimately he wants to control the world so as to punish it.

The only other member of the terrorist group who is similarly motivated is Liputin. In many ways, Liputin is very similar to Stepan Trofimovich. He is contemporary in terms of age; he also holds liberal and atheistic views. Like Stepan Trofimovich, he is also extremely vain in terms of his "progressive" identity. In fact, one of the few times we see Liputin become offended, it is when Stepan Trofimovich tells him that his views are lukewarm insofar as the fact that he represents the "golden mean."

This progressive vanity is displayed in the extreme in one instance, when Nikolai Vsevolodovich openly flirts with and then kisses Liputin's wife. After his wife had feinted with fright, Liputin responds by running to see Nikolai down the stairs and hands him his fur jacket, bowing obsequiously throughout. The following day he sends cordial greetings to Nikolai, expecting him to state that Liputin is the, "wisest man in the whole town." (10:41)

This strange story is but a prelude to a more complete understanding of Liputin as a deeply conflicted man. On the one hand, he is initially described as an elderly, strict, and stingy family man with three adult daughters who works as a provincial official. At the same time, he is an avid disciple of the French utopian philosopher Charles Fourier, whose radicalism contrasts sharply with Liputin's day-to-day mundane provincial existence. It is with Fourier that we find a clue to his strange behavior.

In his writings, Fourier denounced "civilization" as hypocritical and corrupt. In its place he sought to implement a "harmonian order," an order organized in such a manner so as to allow individuals of like passions to associate freely together. The consequent synergy of passions among the members of society results in the complete fulfillment of each individual's passions and economic productivity increases.[4]

Fourier argued that all true human passions are harmonizable. He likened this playing out of individual passions to an orchestra—each player playing his or her part in creating the whole. He explains, "When this social mechanism shall be tested, it will be seen that the passions are all good as God created them, and that when normally developed, they tend to social unity and harmony."[5]

The key challenge in constructing the harmonian society is tied to its organization. The basic organizational building block of the new "harmonian order" is the phalanstery, a four-hundred-person dwelling/work area, in which individuals are carefully matched so as to allow mutual attraction to occur. Because of this concord of passions, interpersonal conflicts disappear and individual contentment is realized.

Fourier believes that the sensual passions, particularly those of touch and taste, are important for the construction of the good society. He writes, "We will learn at last that passionate attraction, accused by our philosophers of vice and corruption, is the wisest and the most admirable of God's works. Passionate attraction alone, without constraint and without aid other than the charm of voluptuousness, is going to establish universal unity upon the globe, and will cause war, revolution, indigence, and injustice to disappear during the seventy thousand year period of social harmony which we will enter."[6]

Indeed, Fourier argues that sensual repression is one of the main problems in his society. He writes, "All repressed passion produces its counter-passion which is malevolent as the natural passion would be beneficial."[7] He recalls a certain Dame Stroganoff, who was renowned for torturing her beautiful slave-girl and hypothesizes that Stroganoff's drive to torture the girl was driven by a suppressed lesbian love. If society had allowed for such a lesbian relationship, Dame Stroganoff could have fulfilled her repressed desires, the girl could have been spared the torture, and in a word they would have, ". . . become very passionate lovers."[8]

Fourier devotes considerable effort in describing specific sensual passions that must be considered in creating harmonian society. He even includes a long exposition on the orgy as a tool in fulfilling man's strong sexual drive and to free him from the negative behavioral results of sexual repression.

Thus, if we place Nikolai Vsevolodovich's scandalous kiss of Liputin's wife in this context, we see that Liputin could not but have accepted this act as anything but Nikolai acting on his own passion. However, there is something more here than this one isolated incident.

Is Liputin attracted to Fourierism, but feels ashamed by his own sexual passions, feeling them to be unusual or perverse? Is it possible that he is attracted to it because through it he is able to conceptualize a life among others who had similar sorts of passions? This would be logical.

The first hint that we have in this regard is the description of Liputin's character. Above all else, he is the novel's most prolific meddler and scandal-monger. He is the character that tells Stepan Trofimovich about Darya's Switzerland-based affair with Nikolai Vsevolodovich. He does this in order to destroy the possibilities of a marriage between the two (he had made Lebyadkin drunk in order to find this out). He also humiliates Lebyadkin by leading him to believe that he can successfully court Lizaveta. Importantly, these scandals revolve around romantic/sexual relations.

Why is he so focused on the immodest relations of others? The hopes of individuals are often a reflection of their own needs. Shigalyov calls for a hierarchical society because he is most comfortable in such a system. Virginsky is sentimental toward others because he knows that he wants others to feel that way about him (particularly his own wife!). Likewise, Liputin tries to shame others through meddling and scandal-mongering because he knows that he is sensitive to the force of shame, particularly with regard to his own intimate relations. It is out of these feelings of vulnerability, that he derives the motivation to shame others with the idea of controlling others.

All of this is clear to Pyotr Stepanovich, who understands how to manipulate this power of shame. As Liputin joins the other four terrorists in challenging his methods, Pyotr cleverly counterattacks, basing his attacks upon Liputin's greatest weakness—his sense of shame. He turns to Liputin and says, "Don't worry, gentlemen, I know all your steps. You're smiling spitefully, Mr. Liputin? Yet I know, for example, that three days ago you pinched your wife all over, at midnight, in your bedroom, as you were going to bed." (10:418) Liputin is stunned at this public revelation and pales. He is ashamed to have this sadistic proclivity displayed in public. This attack effectively silences him.

Pyotr Stepanovich shames Liputin again shortly after this confrontation. After the above-mentioned meeting with his terrorist cell had concluded, Pyotr sets out to meet with Kirillov. On the way, he stops for a bite to eat. The narrator writes that Pyotr does not allow Liputin to walk alongside of him on the narrow sidewalk. In fact, he pays no attention to him whatsoever. This treatment enrages Liputin to such a degree that it "took his breath away." (10:422) The narrator continues that Liputin had begun hating him long ago, ". . . not for the danger, but for the arrogance of his treatment." (10:422) However, in spite of this, Liputin knows that he would, "like a slave," be the first to arrive at the spot of the murder of Shatov. In other words, even though he was resentful, he was obedient. Indeed, when the time for the murder does arrive, unlike Shigalyov, who walks away, or Virginsky who does not actively participate, Liputin "threw himself at him from the front [of Shatov]." (10:460) In other words, the force guiding Liputin is not only powerful enough to actively participate in the murder, but he does so in full view of the victim's face.[9]

Because Pyotr Stepanovich realizes that this force of shame is the most powerful force in his psychological quiver, he uses it in group scenarios as well. In yet another rather remarkable scene, Pyotr leads a meeting of local radicals at Virginsky's house. Throughout the meeting he remains aloof, if not downright rude. In the midst of the meeting he asks for a deck of cards, followed by a glass of cognac, and then lastly scissors for cutting his nails. (10:307-308) In behaving in such a manner, he is trying to shame them by treating them in an aloof manner. After all, this is a meeting of revolutionaries who pride themselves on their ideas. By writing off their ideas so casually, he is shaming them. In order to avoid shame, they will need to prove themselves to him.

Importantly, Liputin's fear of shame is sufficiently strong so as to maintain his loyalty to "the cause" over the long term. Liputin is willing to kill in order to avoid not being loved (i.e., shamed). Perhaps more significantly, he is also motivated to commit this act in the hope of helping to build that future "harmonian" society. When Liputin learns just after the murder that he is a part of the only group of five in the world, it sows the first seeds of doubt. However for the following two weeks he behaves in a perfectly predictable manner for someone so strongly motivated. He escapes to St. Petersburg, obtains a false passport, as well as the money and means to escape abroad. For two weeks he unsuccessfully looks for Nikolai Vsevolodovich and Pyotr Stepanovich. After two weeks he suddenly goes on a binge. He seeks solace in a brothel, a location where he could pursue his unique passions. Importantly, he is found there drunk. We may conjecture from this drunkenness that he was attempting to mollify his guilty conscience through the bottle.

Dostoevsky clearly indicates through this that the force of shame is more powerful than the force of sentiment, which in turn is more powerful than the force of hierarchy. Not only did Liputin remain loyal and clear-headed for two weeks, but even after his capture, he remained loyal to his utopian dream. The narrator reminds us that he, ". . . is preparing for the approaching trial somewhat triumphantly and hopefully (?). He even intends to make a speech at the trial." (10:512)

The Scum People

How then are we to explain the remaining two terrorists, Lyamshin and Tolkatchenko? Upon initial inspection these two have no particular motivation but mischief. To state it differently, they appear to be naturally drawn to trouble. Our narrator explains it as follows:

> Always and everywhere, in a troubled time of fluctuation or transition, various trashy sorts appear. I am not speaking of the so-called "vanguard," who always rush ahead of everyone else (their main concern) and whose goal, though very often quite stupid, is still more or less definite. No, I am speaking only of scum. This scum, which exists in every society, rises to the surface in any transitional time, and not only has no goal, but has not even the inkling of an idea, and itself merely expresses with all its might anxiety and impatience. And yet this scum, without knowing it, almost always falls under the command of that small band of the "vanguard" which acts with a definite goal. . . (10:354)

What needs to be remembered about these two characters is that they are every bit as human as the other three "vanguard" terrorists, with the same basic human needs. More specifically, Dostoevsky creates characters here that share the need to be loved. Shigalyov seeks love through his hierarchy; Virginsky through his worldly caring sentiment; Liputin through the avoidance of being hated and shamed. These latter two terrorists seek love and admiration through clownishness (Lyamshin) and provocation (Tolkatchenko).

Throughout the novel we learn very little about Tolkatchenko. He is only first mentioned halfway through the novel and very little attention is given to him thereafter. To the Russian-reading audience, the first impression of this character is based upon his name, which evokes a thoroughly roguish quality. The verb *tolkat'*, which is the root of the name, in Russian means to instigate, incite, or provoke.

Consistent with this image as an instigator, we learn that he is knowledgeable about the peasants, and a particular authority on thieves and robbers. The feeling we get about him is that he frequents taverns not only because he can study his subjects there, but that he has base desires. We also learn that he takes pride in his shabby dress, speaks with peasant phrases, and much like Lyamshin, wears tarred boots.

Tolkatchenko interprets the attention given to him for his antics as love and admiration. His key weakness is his fear of being arrested. Knowing this, Pyotr Stepanovich has leverage over him. As Tolkatchenko joins the others in questioning his leadership of the group after the burning of the town, Pyotr responds by reminding him that he had been inciting the peasant Fomka Zavyalov in the "forget-me-not" pub the day before the fire. This fear is used by Pyotr Stepanovich to keep Tolkatchenko quiet.

The character of Lyamshin is a shameless post-office clerk/revolutionary who takes great pleasure in playing the fool. He entertains others by playing the piano, imitating the sound of a pig, and walking on his hands. He also entertains by committing practical jokes. He is a buffoon who secretly slips obscene photographs into the bag of a gospel-woman and who releases a mouse into the empty slot of a recently stolen icon. He is also the clown who eats from a cluster of grapes taken from the plate of a young man who had just committed suicide.

Much like Tolkatchenko, Lyamshin interprets the attention given to him in the midst of his antics as love and admiration. However, unlike with Tolkatchenko, Pyotr Stepanovich does not know how to leverage this psychological trait in the service of his activities. Pyotr explains that, "Liputin is a crook, but I know his specific critical point (*tochka*). There is not a crook that does not have his specific critical point. Lyamshin is the only one who hasn't, but he is in my hands." (10:322) Indeed, Lyamshin's most serious concern up to the murder appears to be with his health—a rather odd concern for a committed revolutionary.

It is therefore not surprising that Lyamshin is the least committed of all those who actually participate in the murder, and the first to crack under the psychological pressure of the act. Near the beginning of the chapter in which the murder of Shatov takes place, we read that Lyamshin is in bed, seriously ill, when Virginsky comes to discuss the plan with him (10:455). Indeed, even the act itself is a problem. Lyamshin joins the murderous group only after the fatal shot is fired and hides behind Virginsky as the others prepare the body for burial in the pond. Suddenly, and quite unexpectedly, Lyamshin utters a sustained, unnatural, "animal-like" shriek while squeezing Virginsky from behind. (10:461) He is only quieted by Erkel, who shoves his scarf into Lyamshin's mouth. Although he regains his composure (and apologizes for the outburst), he slips into a long-term depression in the following days. While being watched by Tolkatchenko and Erkel, he calmly spends the following day lying in his bed with his face turned to the wall not uttering a word. After unsuccessfully attempting suicide, he eventually runs to the authorities and informs them of the entire series of events leading to the murder of Shatov, the death of Kirillov, and the deaths of the Lebyadkins.

Implication: The Cementing Force

Pyotr Stepanovich cleverly manipulates the forces of the uniform, sentiment, and shame in order to manage his terrorist cell. He suspects, however, that they are not powerful enough to motivate individuals within his group to operate over an extended period of time. He needs an even more powerful force—one that can more effectively propel the group forward in its destructive trajectory.

This is provided by Nikolai Vsevolodovich, who suggests to Pyotr that the group kill off one of its own members so as to implicate all of them in a murder. He explains, "All this hierarchy and sentimentality—it is good glue, but there is one thing better still: convince four members of a circle to bump off a fifth on the pretense of his being an informer, and with this shed blood you will immediately tie them together in a single knot. They will become your slaves, they would not dare rebel or call you to accounts." (10:299)

It is of considerable importance that Nikolai Vsevolodovich does not suggest a single specific person. A great deal has been made in the secondary literature about the symbolic importance of the fact that Shatov is a Slavophile; that, by killing Shatov, the terrorists are symbolically killing Russia and Russian traditions. The case for this is enhanced by the fact that the terrorists did not select as their target Lebyadkin, the individual who represents a far greater threat to the cell. After all, he actually sends a letter to the Governor denouncing them.

What is of greater interest to us at this point is the fact that the power of implication is not a new idea to Pyotr Stepanovich at the time that Nikolai Vsevolodovich tells him about it. We actually see Pyotr attempt to use this technique in the scene in which Pyotr visits Nikolai as the latter is recovering from the blow which Shatov had dealt him. Pyotr understands that the one thing impeding the marriage between Nikolai and Lizaveta Nikolaevna is his secret marriage to Marya Lebyadkina. He tells Nikolai, ". . . I am seriously at your service, always and everywhere and in any circumstance—I mean any, understand?" (10:179) Pyotr adds that a former serf of his, Fedka the Convict, is in town and that he is a man ready, "for anything, anything—for money . . . if you were serious just now about that plan, remember, to do with Lizaveta Nikolaevna, then I repeat once more that I, too, am a man ready for anything, in all senses, whatever is useful to you, and am completely at your service." (10:181) When he receives no response, he hurries to leave, but blurts out that Fedka could also be of use in taking care of other people as well, such as Gaganov or Shatov. Pyotr is not merely just trying to help Nikolai, but attempting to implicate Nikolai in a crime of murder.

Just as he uses the force of implication on Tolkatchenko, Pyotr Stepanovich also uses the force of implication to get the entire group of five to cooperate in the murder of Shatov. Pyotr Stepanovich burns down the town in order to compel the cell members to kill Shatov. Pyotr explains to them, "They will arrest you not only as inciters to arson, but as a fivesome. The informer knows the whole secret of the network." (10:419) He then proceeds to claim that Shatov is the informer.

This proved to be highly effective at getting the group of five to at least show up for the murder of Shatov. Dostoevsky explains, "That Shatov would denounce them all our people believed; but that Pyotr Stepanovich was playing with them like pawns—they also believed. And, what is more, they all knew that they would still come together to the spot the next day, and that Shatov's fate had already been decided. They felt they had suddenly been caught like flies in the web of a huge spider; they were angry but quaking with fear." (10:421)

The Fifth (and Chief) Force: Nihilism

The repulsiveness of Pyotr Stepanovich's snake-like and spider-like motivational techniques are effective in the short term. Ultimately, he successfully uses them to motivate most of his terrorist cell members to participate in the murder of the innocent Shatov. He comes to the conclusion, however, that these techniques will not work in the long run. He also correctly concludes that he lacks the personal leadership qualities necessary to compensate for the weaknesses of his motivational techniques. Such obviously repulsive people can never effectively lead people in the long haul. It is for this reason that Pyotr Stepanovich is not a "clever" or "subtle" serpent. Nikolai Vsevolodovich is. Nikolai is never banal or repulsive. In fact, he is strangely appealing to others.

Pyotr Stepanovich recognizes this and pleads with Nikolai Vsevolodovich by imploring him to instruct him, ". . . how to act." (10:319) He says to Nikolai: "You are the chief, you are the force; I will only be at your side, as a secretary." (10:299) It is not so much that Pyotr needs Nikolai to teach him how to deceive people (through psychological enticement or implication). He already knows how to do that. What is it exactly that he needs?

Pyotr Stepanovich gives us a clue when he makes the following impassioned speech to Nikolai Vsevolodovich, just after he had abruptly walked out of Pyotr's revolutionary meeting:

> Stavrogin, you are beautiful! . . . Do you know that you are beautiful! The most precious thing in you is that you sometimes do not know it. . . . There is even simple heartedness and naivety in you, do you know that? . . . I love beauty. I am a nihilist, but I love beauty. Do nihilists really not love beauty? They just do not love idols, but I love an idol! You are my idol! You do not insult anyone, yet everyone hates you; you have the air of being everyone's equal, yet everyone is afraid of you—this is good. . . . You are precisely what is needed. I, I need precisely such a man as you. I know no one but you. You are a teacher, you are a sun, and I am your worm. . . . (10:324)

Pyotr is a self-proclaimed nihilist—and yet he declares Nikolai to be his idol. By definition, a nihilist can not have an idol—or an ideal. This is precisely the point. Nikolai is the embodiment of nihilism. It is only with nihilism that Pyotr can build his Shigalyovian world through terrorism.[10] Pyotr is ready to make Nikolai into "Ivan the Tsarevich" while he remains his secretary. (10:325)

Nikolai is not just nihilistic, he is beautiful. He not only rejects traditional morality, but he can convince others to do it by making it look good. Like the clever serpent of the Garden of Eden, he is able to lure people into committing acts they may not normally do through attraction. He can convince them to eat of the forbidden tree of knowledge by making it a, "delight to the eyes."[11]

Nikolai Vsevolodovich's beauty is not purely physical, it is symbolic. As a nihilist, Nikolai represents extreme freedom. As a symbol of complete freedom, he is attractive to others. Pyotr Stepanovich needs Nikolai because the vision of complete freedom is far more attractive than is the vision of complete equality that Pyotr supposedly stands for. In order for Shigalyovian equality to be truly realized, the extreme freedom of nihilism must be promised (but not delivered). Nikolai Vsevolodovich will be the pretender, the "Ivan the Tsarevich," in his new Shigalyovian world.

It is in this way that nihilism is seen by Pyotr Stepanovich as the most powerful of all the forces that can motivate an effective terrorist. For him, the ability to convince others to commit remorseless murder is the most effective tool a terrorist manager can have. He refers to it as the "most precious" thing, when, at the moment at which Nikolai appears to be leaving for good. Pyotr is described with the following words: "This was a man still stunned because his most precious thing was being, or had already been, taken away." (10:321) Indeed, so long as terrorists have feelings of remorse over the pain and suffering they cause, there is little hope that they can operate efficiently in the long run. Nihilism seems, to Pyotr, to be a perfect solution to this problem.

The Paradox of Terroristic Nihilism

On the surface, nihilism is seductively attractive. It represents complete freedom: freedom of action and freedom from conscience. By creating the purely nihilistic character of Nikolai Vsevolodovich, Dostoevsky ingeniously illustrates however the paradox of this freedom. While it frees individuals to act in any manner they so desire, it does not propel them to act in the name of any particular ideal. Without ideals one is freed from conscience, but without a conscience one is freed from ideals. Without ideals, one can not have a cause. It is through Nikolai that Dostoevsky illustrates this striking paradox.

In his last letter to Darya Pavlovna, Nikolai is surprisingly direct about this paradox. He warns her by writing, "No, you had better be more careful: my love will be as shallow as I myself am, and you will be unhappy. Your brother told me that he who loses his ties with his own soil also loses his own gods, that is, all his purposes. One can argue endlessly about everything, but what poured out of me was only negation, with no generosity and no force." (10:514)

With this confession he isolates the source of his nihilism—the abandonment of his "gods." Without the gods or ideals, all that he has left are "shallow" sentiments. He can not love, nor can he feel. Can any human being live the soulless existence absent the sentiments? Dostoevsky does not believe so. For him, death is a welcome release from the emptiness of a soulless life.

It is not coincidental that Dostoevsky makes Nikolai Vsevolodovich a fearless character. Because death is seen in the positive light of a release from a burdensome life, a soulless creature would logically feel no fear of death. As the narrator describes,

> Nikolai Vsevolodovich was one of those natures that feels no fear. In a duel he would stand cold-bloodedly before his adversary's fire, take aim himself, and kill with brutal calm. If anyone had slapped him on the cheek then, I think he would not even have challenged the offender to a duel, but would have killed him at once, on the spot. . . . I even think that he never knew those blinding fits of anger that make one unable to reason. (10:164)

The flip side of this is that the soulless man has no reason to continue living. Suicide is insignificant to an individual who has a dead soul. Indeed, to make it perfectly clear that it was not some sort of psychological anomaly that results in Nikolai's suicide, Dostoevsky ends the novel with this one sentence: "Our medical men, after the autopsy, completely and emphatically ruled out insanity." (10:516)

We may therefore conclude that for Dostoevsky nihilism is an impractical belief-system for a terrorist. The same can be said about the force of the uniform, the force of sentimentality, and the force of implication. Indeed, according to Dostoevsky, the terrorist manager seems left with very few motivational tools. Of those listed by Pyotr Stepanovich, only one seems to have the staying power necessary for continuing terrorist operations—the force of shame. As we shall see in our final chapter, it is to this force that Dostoevsky devotes his last novel—*The Brothers Karamazov.*

Notes

1. For insight here see, Carolyn Heilbrun, "The Character of Hamlet's Mother," *Shakespeare Quarterly* 8, No. 2 (Spring 1957): 201-206. Some scholars have argued that Gertrude is dull, shallow, and immature.

2. Dostoevsky mentions three times that he has long ears. Joseph Frank correctly points out that in the notebooks for *The Demons*, Shigalyov is modeled upon Russian revolutionary nihilist V. A. Zaitsev, who is reputed to have had long ears. See Joseph Frank, *Dostoevsky: The Miraculous Years, 1865-1871* (Princeton, N.J.: Princeton University Press, 1995): 449. See also Tibor Szamuely, *The Russian Tradition* (London: Fontana Press, 1988): 325-327.

3. Michael Katz accurately translates *obshchechelovek* as "universal humanitarian." This is the most accurate of all English-language translations that have yet to appear. See Fyodor Dostoevsky, *Devils* (Oxford: Oxford University Press, 1992): 235.

4. Charles Fourier, *Harmonian Man: Selected Writings of Charles Fourier*, ed. Mark Foster, trans. Susan Hanson (Garden City, New York: Doubleday, 1971)

5. Charles Fourier, *Harmonian Man: Selected Writings of Charles Fourier*, 190.

6. Charles Fourier, *Harmonian Man: Selected Writings of Charles Fourier*, 90.
7. Charles Fourier, *Harmonian Man: Selected Writings of Charles Fourier*, 75.
8. Charles Fourier, *Harmonian Man: Selected Writings of Charles Fourier*, 75.
9. It seems quite likely that Dostoevsky has Pyotr Stepanovich understand this as "the most powerful force" primarily because it exercises an enormous force upon him. Indeed, the fear of humiliation is so significant for Pyotr Stepanovich that he feels "rage which takes his breath away" when he remembers how he had gone, ". . . scurrying through the mud" behind Nikolai Vsevolodovich in precisely the same way as he forced Liputin to do so.
10. Nikolai understands that many are attracted to him for this reason and even complains at one point that everyone is convinced that he could play the role of Stenka Razin, a Cossack rebel of the seventeenth century.
11. For devout Christians, like Dostoevsky, this is the *modus operandi* of demons as well. Demons, theologically speaking, are dangerous because they can convince normally virtuous people to sin by deceiving them into believing that a certain action is "good."

Chapter 6
Demonic Shame

Dostoevsky spent most of his life attempting to understand and describe the abyss of nihilism. He was not the first to do so; this was a preoccupation of many continental philosophers of the nineteenth century. He was also not the most famous thinker to do so; Friedrich Nietzsche surely gains this honor. Dostoevsky's contribution in this regard seems to revolve around his ability to *synthesize* the cultural, political, and psychological aspects of this nihilistic abyss.

Up to this point, we have discussed all three of these aspects. In chapter 2 we examined the cultural aspect of enlightenment rationalism as it appeared within a new culture of Parisian cosmopolitanism. In chapter 3 we examined the political road that Dostoevsky felt led from cosmopolitan egalitarianism to democratic despotism. In chapter 4 we examined the psychological road from cosmopolitan vanity to nihilistic rage. Finally, in chapter 5 we examined the uselessness of nihilism as a tool for terrorism, but found that the psychology of shame can function as a powerful, and violent, force for the humiliated.

For most readers, this final point feels like a hanging thread—a small, but annoying flaw on an otherwise exquisite form. In point of fact, this final point is not inconsequential. As will be recalled, almost all of the characters found in *The Demons* end the novel in death, suicide, jail, or abandonment. Importantly, they all end as devastated and broken people. There are two important exceptions to this: Pyotr Stepanovich, the terror-cell leader who successfully eludes the Russian authorities, and Liputin, who remains convinced of the rightness of the cause while in jail preparing his own legal defense. Why does Dostoevsky conclude in this way? What is he saying about the uniqueness of the two characters?

The key to understanding this lies in the immense power of shame. It will be recalled that the two terrorist cell members motivated to act out of a sense of shame were none other than Liputin and Pyotr Stepanovich.[1] In chapter 3 we saw how a shunned and abandoned Pyotr Stepanovich developed into a resentfully shamed young man. In chapter 5 we saw how he manipulated Liputin based upon this same fear of shame.

Clearly, shame is an important psychological force for Dostoevsky. However, in *The Demons* he offers an incomplete analysis of it. Godless culture, politics, and psychology are the themes of *The Demons*, but the role of shame is only lightly touched upon. Dostoevsky seems to have felt that an additional step must be taken in this regard. He felt that it was necessary to examine how shame and nihilism interact to create an extremely volatile brew. This is precisely what he did in his next, and final, novel—*The Brothers Karamazov*. In this sense, *The Brothers Karamazov* is a novel about godless, or demonic, shame.

Degrees of Shame

In his classic work on Dostoevsky, Edward Wasiolek observed that the name of the town in which most of the action of *The Brothers Karamazov* takes place is *Skotoprigonevsk*, a name derived from the Russian word for "beast pen."[2] He suggests that the Karamazov home is the center of the human corruption illustrated in the novel. A character's relative level of corruption is in direct proportion to the distance that he lives from this corrupt center. Here we will take a somewhat different tact; we will argue that the greater the degree of shame experienced by a character, the more prone that individual will be to violence.

Various degrees of shame are experienced by the main characters of this novel.[3] Let us first begin with the basic story line of the novel. The action of this novel centers upon the Karamazov family—a family consisting of a father (Fyodor) and four sons (Dmitri, Ivan, Alyosha, and Smerdyakov). We first meet these characters at the very beginning of the novel as they meet for a family mediation session at the town's monastery. The meeting has been set in order to establish peaceful relations between Fyodor and his eldest son Dmitri, who feels that he has not only been cheated out of his inheritance by his father, but that his own father is attempting to woo away the woman with whom he has fallen in love (Grushenka). Ironically, Dmitri feels that he needs his inheritance money in order to run off and marry Grushenka. Fyodor intends to use this money to entice and seduce the very same Grushenka.

The first scene at the monastery ends with no resolution of the conflict. Fyodor and Dmitri seem to be on a collision course over the money and the common love interest. At one moment during the meeting, Dmitri significantly cries out in rage: "Why is such a man alive? . . . Tell me, can he be allowed to go on dishonoring the earth?" (14:69)

Upon the completion of the first scene, we learn that Dmitri had taken money from another of the town's inhabitants (Katerina) with the promise that he would forward it to her relatives in Moscow. Rather than forwarding the money, he squandered half of the money by entertaining peasants and gypsies in a nearby town. To further complicate the matter, we also learn that he is formally engaged to Katerina, but not in love with her. Dmitri's obsession is with the aforementioned Grushenka.

Immediately upon squandering this money, Dmitri feels remorse for having "stolen" Katerina's money and embarks upon a series of adventures in an effort to pay this money back. After failing to get money from the last of a series of individuals in town (a certain Madame Khokhlakov), he snatches up a pestle and runs from her home. Pestle in hand, he resolves to take the money from his father (he does not feel that he is "stealing it" as he considers it his inheritance). The fact that this money is promised by his father to the object of his obsession—Grushenka—is, of course, salt in the wounds.

Upon arriving at his father's house, he sees him within. However, at the moment that he may have struck, Gregory, the old servant who had raised him, emerges from his small house in the yard. Gregory sees Dmitri and attempts to chase him off. Dmitri hits Gregory with the pestle, and thinking that he had killed him, flees. Dmitri then travels to the nearby town of Mokroe, the town to which Grushenka had just traveled with her long-standing fiancé (who had unexpectedly turned up in town). Dmitri's intention is not only to see her, but to throw a party. This is to be his last hurrah, as he is certain to be arrested and imprisoned for his earlier assault/murder of Gregory. At the inn, he meets up with Grushenka's party and manages a reconciliation with her. Shortly thereafter, he is arrested and charged with the murder of his father (not the murder of Gregory, who had only been injured by the pestle blow). The rest of the novel is devoted to the court proceedings involving the murder of his father.

In the course of the investigation and trial, it is learned that Dmitri actually suspects Smerdyakov of the murder. As the story continues to unfold, we learn that he is indeed the murderer. On the evening of the murder, just after Dmitri had escaped his father's yard, Smerdyakov snuck into Fyodor's house and murdered him, taking the 3,000 rubles that Dmitri had claimed as his inheritance in order to implicate his older brother. The novel ends with Dmitri's conviction of the crime of patricide, Ivan's slide into insanity, and Smerdyakov's suicide. Only Alyosha is left alive, whole, and for the most part, composed.

So how does all of this relate to Dostoevsky's conception of how an individual can be led to commit the violent crime of patricide? As mentioned in chapter 1, shame can be defined as the withdrawal of love. Shame experienced as a child can be particularly devastating. Ultimately, this can end in violence. It will be argued here that the role of shame is critical in understanding the motivations of these characters. In order to answer this question we must look carefully at the characters of the four sons in order to determine if this approach fits with Dostoevsky's depiction of the brothers Karamazov and their upbringing.

Dmitri Karamazov—The Sensualist

The portrait Dostoevsky draws of the parenting skills of Fyodor Karamazov is not a terribly flattering one. It turns out that Fyodor, a "landowner," had been married twice and that Dmitri is his son by the first marriage. After his first wife had left him, Fyodor functionally abandons the son he had by her (Dmitri), and slips into a dissipated lifestyle for a good period of time. Dmitri is essentially raised by the household servant Gregory. Several years later, Fyodor married again, a marriage which produced two more sons—Ivan and Alyosha. This marriage, however, does not reform the corrupt lifestyle that Fyodor embraced after his first wife had left. He collects together loose women in his house and openly held orgies in his wife's presence. She died after eight tortuous years.

If all of this behavior is not despicable enough, Dostoevsky has Fyodor sink to even lower levels of moral debauchery. Having drunkenly boasted of his ability to seduce the town's mentally retarded homeless woman (Lizaveta), he ends upon fathering a fourth son by her. She dies in childbirth. Gregory, the same servant charged with raising the other sons, now takes on yet another Karamazov son to raise. Eventually, this last son—nicknamed Smerdyakov—is made Fyodor's cook.

In sum, Fyodor abandons all of his sons in the novel, but the degree of rejection varies.[4] Fyodor fights with his eldest son, but does not seem to have rejected him emotionally. To state it another way, he is not ashamed of Dmitri. He does, however, several things to humiliate him. Not only does he abandon him—an abusive act in itself—but he attempts to steal away the one woman with whom he has an obsession. Because of this abandonment, and the complete lack of a mother figure, the reader is left to conclude that Dmitri has a serious deficit of familial love.

In order to compensate for this, Dmitri seeks love in another individual who, like him, has a history of abandonment and lack of self-love—Grushenka. His obsession with her becomes clear very early in the novel when he states that he will be her husband under any circumstance. He states, ". . . when [her] lover comes, I'll go into the next room. I'll clean her friends' dirty galoshes, light their samovar, run their errands." (14:110) When Dmitri learns that Grushenka's first love (a Polish gentleman) had returned to town and taken her away, he responds by stating, "She's now with him. . . . Now I shall see what she looks like with him . . . [and then] I will disappear." (14:370)

Dmitri is capable of treating people both callously and caringly. His love of Grushenka is balanced by his callous treatment of the woman to whom he is formally engaged—Katerina. In yet another scene, which will be discussed in greater depth shortly, he also cruelly humiliates a retired military man in front of his pleading son. Dostoevsky has this event play a pivotal role leading to the illness and death of this young boy.

A careful reading of *The Brothers Karamazov*, however, indicates that this character has more depth than that of a simple bipolar violent lover. Dostoevsky portrays Dmitri as exuding an intense sadness that he is attempting to disguise or sublimate through sensuality. The narrative states, "Others, who saw something pensive and sullen in his eyes were startled by his sudden laugh, which revealed light-hearted thoughts while his eyes seemed so gloomy." (14:63)

Indeed, Dmitri is not your average scoundrel. He very much seems to have his own code of honor. For instance, he does not want to be considered a thief and goes to great lengths to reimburse Katerina for the money he had squandered. It was this self-loathing shame of being a thief that leads to the uncontrollable rage that compels him to senselessly attack Captain Snegiryov, the father of the aforementioned humiliated boy.

So how can we explain Dmitri's actions? Dmitri seems to have every reason to harbor anger toward the father who had emotionally abandoned him, who had withdrawn his inheritance, and who was threatening to steal the object of his love obsession. It is only natural that these two characters would have such violent quarrels. Dostoevsky seems to be indicating here that this is an individual who is seeking love, both from his father as well as from a woman. The father seems intent on withholding his own love, and keeping his son from having it with another. In essence, Dmitri is love-starved and his father is acting to obstruct Dmitri in his efforts to find it.

Dostoevsky conveys this message in a shockingly unexpected act that occurs near the beginning of the novel. Upon the completion of the family mediation meeting at the town's monastery, it will be recalled that Father Zosima, the wise mediator, bowed to a very ill-mannered and ill-behaved Dmitri until his forehead touched the floor. What Zosima is trying to convey to Dmitri is that he respects and loves him. Zosima, in essence, identifies Dmitri's need for love and, in his own way, tries to fulfill some of his psychological need through this sign of respect.

Can an individual like Fyodor, who is in a position to keep a person like Dmitri from being loved so provoke his son so as to compel him to patricide? While Dmitri on repeated occasions makes such threats against his father, it appears by the end of the novel that he is probably not capable of such a crime.

Ivan Karamazov—the Intellectual

Ivan, the older of the two children that Fyodor bore with his second wife, is the intellectual of the family, a trait he showed from a very young age. By the time he was a young man, he had become known in literary circles through the publication of brilliant articles and book reviews. In one article, Ivan discusses the appropriate role of the ecclesiastical courts. In this piece, he argues that, ". . . every earthly State should be, in the end, completely turned over to the Church and should become nothing else but a Church, rejecting every purpose incongruous with the aims of the Church." (14:58) Members of the Church faction regarded Ivan as their ally in the battle with the atheists, while the atheists thought that the article was nothing more than, ". . . an impudent farce and mockery." (14:16) If it was love and respect that Ivan was looking for in the publication of this piece, he seems to have been supremely successful.

Ivan represents for Dostoevsky the rationalist product of West European utilitarianism. Like Turgenev's Bazarov, he is a nihilist who believes in neither God nor morality. He only believes in utility and empiricism. At one memorable point in the novel he explains to his younger brother, ". . . I have a Euclidian, earthly mind and so therefore I can not solve problems that are not of this world. And I advise you never to think about it either, my friend Alyosha, especially about God, whether He exists or not. All such questions are utterly inappropriate for a mind created with an idea of only three dimensions." (14:214)

Ivan's adherence to West European utilitarianism, however, is somewhat ambivalent. While he adheres to this "three dimensional" approach to understanding the world, he also seems to hint that this approach is potentially flawed. In one of his most famous statements, he declares, "I want to travel from here to Europe, Alyosha. And yet I know that I am only going to a graveyard, but it is a most precious graveyard . . . I know I shall fall on the ground and kiss those stones and weep over them even though I'm convinced in my heart that it has long been nothing but a graveyard." (14:210) In other words, Ivan knows that by embracing utilitarianism and empiricism he embraces a "dead" set of European ideals.

Ivan's intellectualism perplexes his father, but does not lead to the same level of conflict as observed with Dmitri. However, much like Dmitri, Ivan suffers from a deficit of familial love. Rather than engaging in carousing and womanizing, he seeks love through prestige and intellectual fame. In other words, he wants people to love and respect him due to his intellect. The divinity student, Rakitin, correctly guesses this when he hypotheses that the atheistic Ivan had written the aforementioned ecclesiastical courts article as a "joke." Rakitin surmises that Ivan's primary goal is to gain the respect of Katerina (Dmitri's fiancé!) through such behavior.

Because Ivan has rejected ideals, he is not able to love. Indeed, he admits this in stating, "One can love one's neighbors in the abstract, or even at a distance, but at close quarters it's almost impossible." (14:216) This is, of course, reminiscent of the aforementioned quote from Rousseau's *Emile*, "Distrust those cosmopolitans who go to great length in their books to discover duties they do not deign to fulfill around them. A philosopher loves the Tartars so as to be spared having to love his neighbors."[5]

Indeed, the cosmopolitan Ivan cannot even love those he *does* know. He clearly wants Katerina to love him, but he is unable to love her. Even more significant is his inability to love his loathsome father. He even admits toward the end of the novel that he actually wanted his father to be murdered by stating, ". . . perhaps I was guilty; perhaps I really had a secret desire for my father's death." (15:66)

Predictably, Ivan is also incapable of loving, "in the abstract." In other words, loving those people he does not know. This is evident when, on his way to his final interview with Smerdyakov, he accidentally collides with a drunken peasant, causing the peasant to fall to the ground. It is immediately evident to Ivan that the peasant has been knocked unconscious by the violent collision and will freeze to death in the winter snow if nothing else is done. In spite of this, he continues on his way to meet with Smerdyakov.[6]

Ultimately, Ivan falsely admits to the murder of his father in an effort to expiate his feelings of guilt over his secret desires to see this murder happen. Of course, many readers might conclude that such morbid desires might come naturally to any individual who is subject to the neglectful abuse to which Ivan was subject. Dostoevsky's intended message here, however, is somewhat more subtle. It must be remembered that Ivan is a cosmopolitan intellectual who rejects traditional morality and customs, particularly those of his homeland. He is also a nihilist, who teaches Smerdyakov that "all things are permitted." (15:67) Ivan does not *literally* kill his father, but by rejecting traditional morality and customs of Russia, he is symbolically killing his roots. His father is, of course, one of his two *literal* biological roots. The conclusion that Ivan comes to is clear: by killing the "gods" of the parents, one is symbolically killing the parents themselves. He cannot embrace Western rationalism/utilitarianism without symbolically committing the horrific crime of patricide. This drives him to insanity.

Alyosha Karamazov—The Spiritualist

Alyosha Karamazov is the only redeeming Karamazov character of this novel. In contrast to his brothers, he is a radiant and healthy young man of nineteen. At the same time he is thoughtful and serene. He is the "spiritual" counterpart to the sensual Dmitri and the intellectual Ivan. This point is made clear by Dostoevsky insofar as Alyosha was, at the time of the story, staying in a monastery preparing for the life of a monk.

Alyosha's spirituality is not purely ethereal; Dostoevsky very much has this brother engage the world as a representative of unconditional Christian love. In fact, Christian love is the key aspect of Alyosha's life. Our author writes that Alyosha is, ". . . simply a lover of humanity." (14:17) This is possible because he embraces ideals (God). He is therefore able to love others and is, in turn, loved by others.

Alyosha's love is unconditional and for everyone—even for his despicable father. Alyosha does not condemn his father's obscene behavior, something his father recognizes when he states, "I feel that you're the only creature in the world who has not condemned me." (14:24) As such, Fyodor finds it quite easy to love this son—and display this love. Within two weeks after Alyosha's return home, Fyodor, ". . . took to embracing him [Alyosha] and kissing him terribly often, with drunken tears, with sentimentality. It was evident that he felt a real and deep affection for him, such as he had never been capable of feeling for anyone before." (14:18-19)

Alyosha's unconditional love seems to be able to touch even the most unlikely characters in the novel. At one point even Grushenka, the temptress found at the center of the novel's romantic scandal, is swayed by his loving power. At one point, she falls on her knees declaring that she had been waiting for someone like him all her life. She then states, "I believed that, nasty as I am, someone would really love me, but not only in a shameful manner." (14:323)

The power of love cannot be underestimated for Dostoevsky. Aside from the metaphysical components of Christian love, he alludes to a very pragmatic effect of love in creating a more harmonious society and happy individuals. Love is the key to breaking the vicious cycle of hate (hate leading to ever deeper levels of hate). In other words, Dostoevsky argues that people hate because they have been hated. Only love can compel haters to stop hating.

Dostoevsky means for Alyosha to be the catalyst for stopping this cycle of hate in the world. He writes that Alyosha's "elder" instructed him, before his death, to go out into the world in order to affect change in the world through love. Within three days of Zosima's death Alyosha proceeds to do precisely this.

This leads us to the pivotal question: why is Alyosha so different? If shame and humiliation are the key elements leading to self-loathing and violence, why is Alyosha not as hateful as the other brothers?

Part of the answer lies with the degree of shame experienced by each brother. Dostoevsky informs us that he was not as psychologically damaged as the other brothers in the process of being abandoned/abused by his parents. Although Alyosha also lost his mother, ". . . he remembered her all his life—her face, her caresses, 'as though she stood living before me.'" (14:18) In fact, one of the first things we learn about Alyosha is that he was actually looking for his mother's grave upon arriving in town.[7]

Perhaps more important, at least from Dostoevsky's perspective, is the fact that Alyosha finds the love that his brothers lack through his faith and love in God. Alyosha is thus immune to the feelings of shame associated with the lack of love. God's love led to self-love and the elimination of shame. For Alyosha, the message is clear: God's love precludes shame, and with no shame there is no violence to follow.

Smerdyakov—The Height of Shame

Quite unlike Alyosha, it is almost impossible to find anything redeeming in the character of Smerdyakov, the illegitimate son of Fyodor Karamazov. His mother was, in Dostoevsky's words, "an idiot girl, who wandered about the streets and was known to the whole town by the nickname of Stinking Lizaveta (Lizaveta Smerdyastchaya)." (14:89) As mentioned above, Fyodor had raped her on a bet. She conceived and gave birth to a baby boy. She died immediately after childbirth and was, thus, unable to tell anyone who the father was.

Gregory, the same servant who had earlier adopted Dmitri, adopted the child and named him Pavel. The town's people immediately began to assign the patronymic Fyodorovich, based upon the presumed father's name. Fyodor found this "amusing" but denied any responsibility. He did, however, invent a nickname for the boy—Smerdyakov ("The Stinker"). This name was not only humiliating in itself, but recalls the name of his raped and humiliated mother. Incredibly, Smerdyakov is the only person that Fyodor Karamazov actually trusts. This misplaced confidence results in Fyodor telling Smerdyakov where he had hidden the three thousand rubles that Dmitri considered his inheritance.

Gregory's treatment of Smerdyakov was also a source of humiliation. At one point Gregory yells at him, "You are not a human being. You emerged from the mildew in the bathhouse. That's what you are." (14:114) Not surprisingly, Gregory observes that the child grew up with, ". . . no sense of gratitude," and that, "he [Smerdyakov] doesn't care for you or me, the monster." (14:114)

Smerdyakov is a most extreme victim of humiliation and shame. He is also the most important character of the novel in displaying the effects of such extreme shame. This shame not only damaged his self-esteem—it destroyed it. This ultimately resulted in rage. One passage is striking in this regard. In describing his humiliation, Smerdyakov states,

> . . . they used to call me a stinking bastard in Moscow. It had reached them from here, thanks to Gregory. Gregory blames me for rebelling against my birth, but I would have welcomed their killing me before I was born so that I might not have come into the world at all. They used to say in the market, and your mother too, that my mother's hair was like a mat on her head, and that she was about five foot and a "wee bit." Why talk of a "wee bit" when they might say "a little bit"? . . . Since childhood when I hear "a wee bit," I am ready to burst with rage. I hate all Russia, Maria Kondratyevna. (14:204-205)

It is only natural to assume that such treatment would manifest itself in certain unique behavioral characteristics. While Smerdyakov displays little interest in cultivating friends or romantic relationships with women, he is quite fastidious with regard to his physical appearance, spending a great deal of his salary on clothes, pomade, and perfumes.[8] He also displays, very early on in his childhood, the classic trait of many modern serial killers. Dostoevsky explains that, "In his childhood he liked to hang cats and bury them with great ceremony. He used to dress up in a sheet as though it were a vestment, and sing and wave some object over the dead cat as though it were a censer." (14:114)

As evidence of his "self-death" and the "numb" sensation that is said to accompany such a state, after murdering his own father, Smerdyakov displays no remorse. He clearly did not kill his own father for the money—he easily sacrifices his financial prize without prompting. It also seems unlikely that he was acting upon Ivan's nihilistic ideas (as Raskolnikov does in *Crime and Punishment*). In killing his father he was lashing out violently at the very source of his humiliation. After doing so successfully, his mission is complete. He kills himself as a result of Ivan's threat to charge him in public with his father's murder—a charge that Smerdyakov knows is lacking in physical evidence. For Smerdyakov, suicide is not a dramatic option. It is nothing more than a merciful release from a numb and burdensome life.

The Ravages of Shame: Ilusha Snegiryov

Dostoevsky felt so strongly about the importance of conveying the message about the ravages of shame that he included two other figures within *The Brothers Karamazov* that illustrate this phenomenon: Father Zosima and Ilusha Snegiryov. Let us begin with Ilusha.

Near the beginning of the novel, Alyosha Karamazov encounters a group of six young students who appear to be feuding with one of the other students. In the course of this encounter, Alyosha inadvertently gets involved in a rock fight that had broken out among the children. After being hit by a rock thrown by the lone child, Alyosha quickly learns that his assailant had recently stabbed a certain Krasotkin with a pen-knife. As Krasotkin would not report the assault to the school authorities, the attacker was not formally punished. The rock fight was the means by which the students in the class were meting out their vigilante justice.

Alyosha ends up confronting the child who had pelted him with a rock, asking him what he had done to deserve such an attack. The child not only does not answer, but continues to attack him with a "rage like a little wild beast." (14:163) Upon completing the attack by biting Alyosha's finger, the child retreats, running up the street wailing.

Shortly after this, Alyosha learns that this child's father, a certain Captain Nikolai Snegiryov, had earlier been attacked by his older brother Dmitri, who had grabbed him by the beard and, "dragged him out into the street in such a humiliating fashion." (14:176) Apparently, the man's son, Ilusha, was there during this incident and had pleaded with Dmitri to cease the attack. Adding to the humiliation, the crowd witnessing this scene laughed in amusement. Upon hearing this story, Alyosha quickly came to the realization that this boy, Ilusha, was the very same boy who had thrown a stone at him and had bitten him on the finger.

The role of public humiliation is the key variable here. Alyosha learns that the public humiliation of Ilusha's father occurred within the context of a whole series of traumatizing events for the young Ilusha. In two different portions of the novel, Ilusha reminds his father how badly Dmitri Karamazov had insulted him. Ilusha was clearly personally traumatized by the scene of his father's humiliation.

Adding further injury to this psychological insult, Ilusha had just experienced the loss of his beloved dog and a general social shunning in school. Apparently, Smerdyakov, whom Ilusha had gotten to know, had taught him a nasty trick. He had told the boy to stick a pin into a piece of bread and throw it to a dog to see what would happen. Ilusha did this to his own dog, Zhuchka, not realizing the harm that would result. Upon eating the bread, the dog yelped and ran away. Ilusha became tortured by remorse, having become convinced that he had killed his beloved pet. Ilusha's best school friend, Kolya, then decided to "teach him a lesson" for doing such a nasty deed, by refusing to associate with the boy. As Kolya was a school leader, this was followed by a general social banishment by all the other schoolchildren. It was at this point that Dmitri attacked his father publicly.

It is within this context that the targets of Ilusha's rage make sense—his fellow pupils, Kolya, and ultimately Alyosha. The shame and humiliation from all of these experiences converted themselves into rage. This rage is then followed by illness, an illness which would eventually result in Ilusha's untimely death.

Dostoevsky further emphasizes the importance of this sub-plot by actually ending the book with Ilusha's funeral. Alyosha calls Ilusha's friends, all of whom had just attended the funeral, and makes a speech in which he insists that all the children present should promise not to forget the lessons learned in their hateful treatment of Ilusha. He states,

> Let us make an agreement, here, at Ilusha's stone, that we will never forget Ilusha and one another. And whatever happens to us later in life, even if we don't meet for twenty years, let us always remember the poor boy at whom we once threw stones. Do you remember, by the bridge? . . . He felt for his father's deeply wounded honor and stood up for him. (15:195)

Upon the conclusion of Alyosha's speech, the boys then shout the very last words of novel, "Hurrah for Karamazov." (15:197)

It is no accident that the novel should end in this way. Clearly, Dostoevsky was trying to convey the very theme which provides the unifying motif of this novel—humiliation and shame can lead to rage and violence and self-death. In this case, shame led to the death of a young, innocent child.

The Healing Power of Love: Father Zosima

If childhood humiliation and shame are so pivotal in this story, how then can Alyosha, who as a child experienced nearly the same shame as his other three brothers, not emerge with the same rage and temptations to violence witnessed in Smerdyakov? The answer to this can be found in the figure of Zosima, the "Elder" figure around which the novel actually begins.

Although not a member of the Karamazov family, he is, in essence the father figure for Alyosha. It will be recalled that Alyosha was studying under Zosima in the monastery with the intention of becoming a monk. At the outset of the novel, Zosima functions as a conciliator for the Karamazov family. His conciliation method is based upon the idea that shame and humiliation lie at the root of the Karamazov family violence. At one point Zosima actually states to Fyodor during this initial interview, "Do not trouble yourself. Make yourself quite at home. And, above all, do not be so ashamed of yourself, for it is from this that all the other things come." (14:40)

How then to conquer the detrimental effects of shame? Zosima counsels Fyodor, "It is written: 'Bear circumspectly and gladly dishonor that cometh upon thee by no act of thine own. Be not confounded and hate not him who hath dishonored thee." (14:84) Later, in his last speech before his death he elaborates, "At some thoughts one stands perplexed, especially at the sight of men's sin, and wonders whether one should use force or humble love. Always decide to use humble love." (14:289) With regard to children, he is even more explicit. He explains:

> Every day and every hour, every minute, walk around yourself and watch yourself, and see that your image is a seemly one. You pass by a little child, you pass by, spiteful, with ugly words, with angry soul; you may not have noticed the child, but he has seen you, and your image, unseemly and dishonorable, may remain in his defenseless heart. You don't know it, but you may have sown an evil seed in him and it may grow, and all because you were not careful before the child, because you did not foster in yourself a careful, actively benevolent love. Brothers, love is a teacher; but one must know how to acquire it, for it is hard to acquire, it is dearly bought, it is won slowly by long labor. For we must love not only occasionally, even the wicked can. (14:289-290)

This statement is followed by what is perhaps Zosima's most famous quote. He asks, "Fathers and teachers, I ask: 'What is hell?' I maintain that it is the suffering of being unable to love." (14:292) It is therefore only through Christian love that one can escape a hell like that found within the Karamazov family. It is this love which allows Alyosha to escape the cycle of hate that is pivotal to the reading of this novel; Ivan, Dmitri, and Smerdyakov continued to live in their own loveless personal hells.

The fact that humility and love can heal the hell of the Karamazov family is nicely symbolized in an event that happens quite early in the novel. It will be recalled, that the novel begins as a conciliation meeting for the Karamazov family; a meeting which goes very badly in the end. The climax of this meeting occurs when, after a series of grievously crude comments and behaviors by Dmitri, Zosima, "distinctly and deliberately bowed down at Dmitri Fyodorovich's feet till his forehead touched the floor." (14:69) He then states, "Forgive me! Forgive me, all of you!" (14:69) This show of humility is a precursor to the end of the great tale found in the chapter, "The Grand Inquisitor," in which the Christ figure kisses the inquisitor who is attempting to prosecute him for heresy. Clearly Dostoevsky is arguing that humility and love are the solutions to the effects of shame and humiliation. How then might we apply this to the study of modern terrorism?

The Shame Model

Is it possible that shame and humiliation, such as was experienced by Smerdyakov, motivate modern terrorists today? This is certainly what Dostoevsky argues in both *The Brothers Karamazov* and *The Demons*. A variety of today's scholars have also made this argument.

Anatol Lieven has recently suggested that humiliation has been a particularly important component in the increasing level of popularity of Islamic fundamentalism in the Islamic world. He writes that the, "humiliation of Arab and Muslim world by Israel is so infuriating to them in part because it is only the last in a long history of defeats starting in the seventeenth century and extending far into the twentieth—overwhelmingly at the hands of the Christian world."[9] This humiliation has resulted in the creation of "radical Muslim responses."[10] Importantly, this response is not unique to the Islamic world. He writes that such reaction can be, ". . . found wherever proud people, with strong but in part irrational traditions, feel defeated or radically unsettled by aspects of Western-dominated modernity."[11] Timothy McVeigh, and members of the Japanese terror group, Aum Shinrikyo, feel themselves to be, "pushed to the cultural and economic margins."[12]

James Gilligan has convincingly pointed out that Osama bin Laden indicated a sense of humiliation when he stated after the September 11 attacks, "What America is tasting now is only a copy of what we have tasted. Our Islamic nation has been tasting the same for more than 80 years, of humiliation and disgrace [contempt]."[13] Indeed, as Brian Jenkins has argued, the coordinated attacks that al-Qaeda seems to favor is in itself indicative of this sense of shame. He writes that their multi-location, synchronized attacks, ". . . do not preclude sheer showmanship, especially when that showmanship may not only bring perverse acclaim from other terrorists but also enhance a leader's reputation among people who feel that they have suffered defeat and humiliation."[14]

Bernard Lewis is perhaps the most famous of this group of scholars who currently point to the role of shame and humiliation. In his book, *What Went Wrong?* he points out that, "For many centuries the world of Islam was in the forefront of human civilization and achievement."[15] During much of the past millennium, the West was seen as a backwater, ". . . as an outer darkness of barbarism and unbelief from which there was nothing to learn and little even to be imported, except slaves and raw materials."[16] And then everything changed. Through a series of military defeats, the leading Islamic power of the time, The Ottoman Empire, began to lose a whole series of military engagements against the Western barbarians (beginning with the Treaty of Carlowitz in 1699).[17] This led many within the Islamic world to experience feelings of shame and humiliation that have only compounded with the passing of time. Lewis explains that,

> The relative weakness of the major Islamic powers had already in a sense been revealed by the first European expansion in Asia, when even small countries like Portugal and the Netherlands were able to establish themselves on the seas and on the coasts in defiance of the Muslim powers. The impotence of the Islamic world confronted with Europe was brought home in dramatic form in 1798, when a French expeditionary force commanded by a young general called Napoleon Bonaparte invaded, occupied, and governed Egypt. The les-

> son was harsh and clear—even a small European force could invade one of the heartlands of the Islamic empire and do so with impunity.[18]

This humiliation, Lewis continues, was aggravated by the fact that the only way in which these French military forces were forced to leave Egypt was not by force of Islamic arms, but by another European power (British military forces).

This pattern of Western military conquest was paralleled in the fields of commerce, technology and other spheres of modernization. Leaders within the Islamic world focused on three areas of endeavor in order to catch-up in terms of modernization—military, economic, and political. All three efforts largely failed. In fact, as Lewis writes, "The twentieth century, particularly the second half, brought further humiliations—the awareness that they were no longer even the first among the followers, but were falling ever further back in the lengthening line of eager and more successful Westernizers, notably in East Asia."[19]

Speak Softly and Carry a Big Stick

Most counter-terrorism strategies adopted within Western democracies attempt to treat only the symptoms of terrorism, rather than the underlying causes of it. This is to say that governments tend to take action against a given terrorist group only after an attack has actually occurred. At that point intelligence agencies investigate and collect relevant intelligence, law enforcement agencies act to interdict and arrest, and militaries act against foreign-based terrorist organizations and state sponsors of terrorism.

If Dostoevsky is correct in that shame and humiliation lie at the motivational root of today's most dangerous terrorists, is he also correct in that these feelings among terrorists and terrorist-producing societies can be mollified through "humble love"? Can the United States act as a Superpower Zosima and through acts of love and humility soothe the shame experienced by societies on the other side of the globe?

At first glance, this appears to be an enormously risky national security strategy to adopt when those acting out of a sense of shame may very well use weapons of mass destruction against those that have shamed them. Furthermore, shame and humiliation appear to be enormously powerful forces, difficult if not impossible to eradicate. After all, even Zosima is unable to lift Fyodor Karamazov out of his shamed and humiliated depravity.

Moreover, the use of "humble love" may also be unworkable as a principle of foreign policy. Governments can not "love," only individual human beings can feel and show such an emotion. More importantly, even if a government is somehow able to feel and show love effectively, is there really anything a government or an individual can do for a shamed and humiliated person or society to help them to regain their self-respect and self-love? Probably not. Once again, even Zosima could not do this.

What seems to be far more workable with regard to government policy involves a restraint from displaying the opposite of "humble love"—contempt. Dostoevsky seems to agree with Rousseau in that cosmopolitans are particularly challenged in this regard. Simply put, cosmopolitans are prone to display attitudes of contempt. The urbane sophisticates of London, Paris, and New York are perceived by the traditional and rural villagers of Egypt, Saudi Arabia, and Pakistan as being snobbish, contemptuous elitists.

It is truly ironic that cosmopolitanism, an ideology which celebrates worldliness and cultural diversity, is perceived by traditional groups in peripheral areas as being exclusionary, condescending, and elitist. This humiliation adds to the shame that the non-cosmopolitan already feels as a result of his "backward" political and economic development. Cosmopolitan governments must recognize that this perception exists and must engage in a continuous and carefully constructed publicity campaign aimed at illustrating how they genuinely value the traditional peoples and cultures of the periphery as well.

Cosmopolitan centers are remarkably well positioned to engage in this sort of campaign. Firstly, these centers are usually home to a large number of recent immigrants from these peripheral areas. Any successful campaign must illustrate how these immigrants have been accepted by their cosmopolitan neighbors and how their traditions have been respected. The experience of recent Muslim immigrants to the United States might provide a good model in this regard.[20]

Cosmopolitan centers are also uniquely well-position to illustrate their commitment to respect and appreciate other traditions in so far as cosmopolitanism at least nominally commits itself to cultural diversity. The challenge here is to make what is often a superficial commitment to cultural diversity a real one. In speaking of Islamic fundamentalist terrorism, Bernard Lewis writes, "To this end, we must strive to achieve a better appreciation of other religious and political cultures, through the study of their history, their literature, and their achievements."[21] Governments can not feel or show "love," but they can show recognition and appreciation.

Conversely, Western governments must avoid, at all costs, activities which can be interpreted as demeaning to the cultures and nations from which terrorists emerge. In this regard, the senseless and demeaning treatment of the prisoners held in the Abu Ghraib detention facility and the Guantanamo Bay Naval Facility were not only ineffective at gaining actionable counter-terrorist intelligence, but significantly increased the perception throughout the Middle East of the contempt with which Americans view Muslims.[22] In fact, it increased support for anti-American terrorists in the same way that the publicity surrounding the British government's torture of IRA detainees at Castlereagh increased the general level of support for the IRA among Catholics in Northern Ireland throughout 1970's.

A prudent approach to maintaining the traditional forms of counter-terrorism security alongside a commitment to winning hearts and minds of the core constituencies within which terrorists operate is not a radical one. It does require, however, a delicate balance between just force and sensitive appreciation. The famous foreign policy advice of Theodore Roosevelt seems appropriate here: speak softly and carry a big stick.

Implications for Counter-terrorism Operations

While the message of *The Brothers Karamazov* may be useful with regard to the "strategic" policies made by national leaders, the somewhat more "tactical" implications of *The Demons* are more useful for the counter-terrorism expert. Such an individual would be wise to pay close attention to the contrast between the characters of Nikolai Vsevolodovich Stavrogin and Pyotr Stepanovich Verkhovensky.

As seen in the previous chapter, Nikolai Vsevolodovich has no earthly desire but to regain his own soul. By committing outrages, he hopes to provoke remorse, and thus regain some sort of emotional feeling. Politically inspired violence (terrorism) is of no interest to him. Pyotr Stepanovich, however, is interested in power, and is willing to use violence in order to achieve it. Because he feels emotion, he is theoretically subject to the burdens of human conscience.

To state it differently, Pyotr Stepanovich has at least a limited sense of right and wrong. The fact that he is resentful toward his father for having neglected him indicates that he feels that Stepan Trofimovich's past behavior was wrong. Where there is the existence of a feeling of "wrong," there must also be the existence of a feeling of "right."

For Dostoevsky, therefore, most terrorists are not nihilists. There are moral limits for most terrorists. A modern illustration of this can be seen with the admission of Khalid Sheik Mohammed, the mastermind of the 9/11 terrorist attacks, that he felt remorse over the deaths of children on that day.[23] However, much like Liputin, he remained committed to his war of terror against the United States.

What this means is that many terrorists find themselves caught in a crisis of conscience. On the one hand they commit violence to right a perceived wrong. On the other hand, they must overcome the moral restrictions involved with killing. For many successful terrorists, the first justification is sufficient in order to commit the first terrorist act. Once the act is completed, however, the conscience may begin to exact a price for the murder of innocent civilians—particularly children.

As seen in the previous chapters, a variety of psychological types, possessing a wide range of motivations, can be drawn to terrorism.[24] Some motivations are stronger than others. Almost all of them are subject to the burden of human conscience. A prudent counter-terrorism operative must keep this in mind and be particularly receptive to the possibilities of terrorists who crack under the burden of a guilty conscience and attempt to defect in an effort to ease this burden. Governments would be prudent, therefore, in facilitating opportunities to defect for such terrorists. Governments must ensure confidentiality so as to preclude retaliation against the defector and/or his family. Furthermore, it must be made clear that defectors will not be treated harshly. Once again, media coverage of the harsh treatment given to the detainees at Guantanamo and Abu Ghraib contributed to a decrease in trust that very likely kept many defections from happening.

Conclusion: Demonic Shame

Dostoevsky, better than any other writer before or since, addressed the two persistent riddles of terrorism. As a first generation observer of terrorism, he came to the conclusion that this movement was the product of *modern* culture, politics and psychology.

For Dostoevsky, the psychological component was particularly important. He felt that modernity created a demonic shame that fueled terrorism. Importantly, the demonic aspect of this phenomenon was neither metaphysical nor theological. The demons he brings to life in his novel are gracious, subtle, cosmopolitan, rational and scientific. They are also murderers, rapists, arsonists, and terrorists.

God did not cast these demons from high. For Dostoevsky, they were created in cosmopolitan Paris. These were the individuals who deified reason, and in so doing, abandoned the ancient sources of morality—the ancient Gods. By replacing the ancient with the modern Gods of atheism, science, and liberalism, modern societies have abandoned any sort of moral constraint that helped to keep violence and tyranny in check. This created the new, modern, nihilistic world. The irony, of course, is that this nihilism finds its roots in the seemingly benevolent culture of cosmopolitanism, a culture which celebrates worldliness and rationalism. In this sense, cosmopolitanism created the nihilistic generation responsible for the first wave of terrorism in Western history.

It is within this context, the very conclusion of our analysis, that we return to the very first words of *The Demons*—its first epigram. It is here that we find the words,

> For the life of me, the path can't be seen,
> We've lost our way, what is to be done?
> It is clear that a demon's leading us about in the field,
> Making us go around in circles.
> ....
> How many are there? Whence are they being driven?
> What are they singing so plaintively?
> Are they burying a household goblin?
> Are they marrying off a witch?
>
> A. S. Pushkin, "The Demons"

These two fragments derive from a poem entitled by Pushkin, *The Demons*. It is a poem that was well-known to the Russian-reading audience of the 1870's. On one level, the poem tells the story of a fierce snowstorm and the feelings of two occupants of a wooden sledge who are caught in this storm. Dostoevsky not only evokes this poem at the beginning of his book, he adopts the poem's title for his novel. The intended message could not be clearer. For Dostoevsky, Pushkin's poem is an allegory in which the snowstorm represents modern cosmopolitan influences that have descended upon the countryside and obliterated the path of Russia's native soil causing individuals to lose their way.[25]

This is, of course, a somber message. It is not, however, without hope. After all, blizzards do end, the snow melts, and the path eventually clears. Indeed, the hopeful tone of this epigram is echoed in the second, Biblical epigram found just below the first. In this epigram, the demons that possessed a man flee into a herd of swine and destroy themselves through drowning. The saved man is then found sitting at the feet of Jesus.

The serious reader of Dostoevsky should perhaps take to heart the hopeful message of these two epigrams. While Dostoevsky burrowed to the root of terrorism, deep within the abyss of nihilism, he also seems to have felt that there was some cause for hope. Spring will come, the path will clear and the demons will cast themselves into the sea. Perhaps it is with this somewhat hopeful message that we should conclude our analysis of what is one of the most horrific products of modernity—terrorism. Indeed, Dostoevsky would very much have wished for us to end on such a hopeful note.

Notes

1. Of course, Nikolai Vsevolodovich Stavrogin was also shamed, but never committed a violent act in the name of a political cause.

2. Edward Wasiolek, *Dostoevsky: The Major Fiction* (Cambridge: MIT Press, 1964): 181.

3. Because of this focus upon the concept of shame, this chapter will discuss all *four* Karamazov brothers. This is in contrast to the conventional approach to this novel which tends to focus only upon the three older/legitimate brothers. By taking into account the fourth—illegitimate—brother we can more accurately conceptualize the pivotal role that shame and humiliation play in leading to the supremely violent act of patricide.

4. All the brothers were approximately as "motherless."

5. Jean-Jacques Rousseau, *Emile or On Education*, Introduction, Translation and Notes by Allan Bloom (New York: Basic Books, 1979): 39.

6. He comes back later, having been emotionally shaken by this interview, and helps the peasant who had not yet expired.

7. Interestingly, Alyosha's father does not remember where his second wife is buried.

8. One can imagine that he was trying to compensate for his public humiliation through a more dignified physical appearance and wardrobe.

9. Anatol Lieven, "The Cold War Is Finally Over: The True Significance of the Attacks," in James F. Hoge, Jr. and Gideon Rose, eds, *How Did This Happen?* (New York: Public Affairs Reports, Council on Foreign Relations, 2001): 299.

10. Anatol Lieven, "The Cold War Is Finally Over: The True Significance of the Attacks," 300.

11. Anatol Lieven, "The Cold War Is Finally Over: The True Significance of the Attacks," 300.

12. Anatol Lieven, "The Cold War Is Finally Over: The True Significance of the Attacks," 300.

13. James Gilligan, "Shame, Guilt, and Violence," *Social Research* 70, no. 4 (Winter 2003): 1162.

14. Brian M. Jenkins, "The Organization Men: The Anatomy of a Terrorist Attack," in James F. Hoge, Jr. and Gideon Rose, eds, *How Did This Happen?* (Public Affairs Reports, Council on Foreign Relations, 2001): 299.

15. Bernard Lewis, *What Went Wrong? Western Impact and Middle Eastern Response* (Oxford: Oxford University Press, 2002): 3.

16. Bernard Lewis, *What Went Wrong? Western Impact and Middle Eastern Response,* 4.

17. Bernard Lewis, *What Went Wrong? Western Impact and Middle Eastern Response,* 23.

18. Bernard Lewis, *What Went Wrong? Western Impact and Middle Eastern Response,* 31.

19. Bernard Lewis, *What Went Wrong? Western Impact and Middle Eastern Response,* 152.

20. Spencer Ackerman, "Religious Protection: Why American Muslims Haven't Turned to Terrorism," *The New Republic* (December 12, 2005).

21. Bernard Lewis, "The Roots of Muslim Rage," *Policy* 17 (Summer 2001-2002): 26.

22. Experience has illustrated that torture rarely produces quality intelligence. See Stephen Budiansky, "Intelligence: Truth Extraction," *The Atlantic Monthly* 295 (June 2005): 32-35.

23. "Verbatim Transcript of Combatant Status Review Tribunal Hearing for ISN 10024," March 10, 2007, U. S. Naval Base Guantanamo Bay, Cuba, 23. Found at http://www.defenselink.mil/news/transcript_ISN10024.pdf

24. Today, most agree with Dostoevsky's observation that terrorists are motivated in a variety of different ways. Rex A. Hudson includes a Dostoevskian epigram in his book which reads, "While nothing is easier than to denounce the evildoer, nothing is more difficult than to understand him." See Rex A. Hudson, *Who Becomes a Terrorist and Why: The 1999 Government Report on Profiling Terrorists* (Guilford, Conn.: Lyons Press, 1999).

25. This gives extra meaning to Nikolai's letter to Lize when he writes, "Your brother told me that he who loses his ties with his own soil also loses his own gods, that is, all his purposes." (10:514)

Bibliography

Ackerman, Spencer. "Religious Protection: Why American Muslims Haven't Turned to Terrorism," *The New Republic*, December 12, 2005.

Anderson, Benedict. *Imagined Communities: Reflections on the Origin and Spread of Nationalism*. New York: Verso, 1983.

Appiah, Kwame Anthony. *Cosmopolitanism: Ethics in a World of Strangers*. New York: Norton, 2006.

Barzun, Jacques. *From Dawn to Decadence: 1500 to the Present*. New York: HarperCollins, 2000.

Belknap, Robert. "Shakespeare and the Possessed," *Dostoevsky Studies*, Volume 5, 1984. http://www.utoronto.ca/tsq/DS/05/063.shtml, 7 March 2007.

Berlin, Isaiah. "Fathers and Children, the Romanes Lecture 1970," 36 in Ivan S. Turgenev, *Fathers and Sons*, trans. Rosemary Edmonds. New York: Penguin, 1985.

———. *The Hedgehog and the Fox: An Essay on Tolstoy's View of History*. London: George Weidenfeld & Nicolson Limited, 1988.

Bloom, Allan. "Jean-Jacques Rousseau," in Leo Strauss and Joseph Cropsey, *History of Political Philosophy, 3rd Edition*. Chicago: University of Chicago Press, 1987.

———. *Love and Friendship*. New York: Simon & Schuster, 1993.

———. *The Closing of the American Mind*. New York: Simon & Schuster, 1987.

Budiansky, Stephen. "Intelligence: Truth Extraction," *The Atlantic Monthly* 295, June 2005.

Byman, Daniel. "Al-Qaeda as an Adversary: Do We Understand Our Enemy?" *World Politics* 56, October 2003.

Crenshaw, Martha. "The Causes of Terrorism." *Comparative Politics* 13, July 1981.

Curle, Richard. *Characters of Dostoevsky: Studies from Four Novels*. New York: Russell & Russell, 1966.

Darnton, Robert. *The Great Cat Massacre and Other Episodes in French Cultural History*. New York: Basic Books, 1984.

Dostoevskij, F. M. *Polnoe Sobranie Sochinenii i Pisem*, 30 vols. Leningrad: Izdatel'stvo "Nauka," 1972-1990.

———. *Demons*, trans. Richard Pevear and Larissa Volokhonsky. New York: Vintage Books, 1994.

———. *Devils*, trans. Michael R. Katz. Oxford University Press, Oxford, 1992.

———. *The Notebooks for* The Possessed, ed., Edward Wasiolek, trans. Victor Terras. Chicago: University of Chicago Press, 1968.

———. The Possessed, *A Novel in Three Parts*. New York: Macmillan Company, 1913.

Ethridge, Marcus E. *The Political Research Experience: Readings and Analysis*. Armonk, N.Y.: M. E. Sharpe, 1990.

Fourier, Charles. *Harmonian Man: Selected Writings of Charles Fourier*, ed. Mark Foster, trans. Susan Hanson. Garden City, N.Y.: Doubleday, 1971.

Frank, Joseph. *Dostoevsky: The Miraculous Years, 186-1871*. Princeton, N.J.: Princeton University Press, 1995.

———. *Dostoevsky: The Seeds of Revolt, 1821-1849*. Princeton, N.J.: Princeton University Press, 1979.

Gellner, Ernest. *Nations and Nationalism*. Ithaca, N.Y.: Cornell University Press, 1983.

Gilligan, James. "Shame, Guilt, and Violence," *Social Research* 70, Winter 2003.

Grossman, Dave. *On Killing: The Psychological Cost of Learning to Kill in War and Society*. Boston: Little, Brown and Company, 1995.

Gurr, Ted R. *Why Men Rebel*. Princeton, N.J.: Princeton University Press, 1971.

Heilbrun, Carolyn. "The Character of Hamlet's Mother," *Shakespeare Quarterly* 8, Spring 1957.

Hoffman, Bruce. *Inside Terrorism*. New York: Columbia University Press, 1998.

Howe, Irving. "Dostoevsky: The Politics of Salvation," in Rene Wellek, ed., *Dostoevsky: A Collection of Critical Essays*. Englewood Cliffs, N.J.: Prentice Hall, 1962.

Hudson, Rex A. *Who Becomes a Terrorist and Why: The 1999 Government Report on Profiling Terrorists*. Guilford, Conn.: Lyons Press, 1999.

Jenkins, Brian M. "The Organization Men: The Anatomy of a Terrorist Attack," in James F. Hoge, Jr. and Gideon Rose, eds. *How Did This Happen?* Public Affairs Reports, Council on Foreign Relations, 2001.

Khatami, Siamak. "Between Class and Nation: Ideology and Radical Basque Ethnonationalism," *Studies in Conflict and Terrorism* 20, 1997.

Krieger, Murray. "Dostoevsky's 'Idiot': The Curse of Saintliness," in *Dostoevsky: A Collection of Critical Essays*, ed. Rene Wellek. Englewood Cliffs, N.J.: Prentice-Hall, 1962.

Laqueur, Walter, ed. *Voices of Terror: Manifestos, Writings and Manuals of Al Qaeda, Hamas, and Other Terrorists from Around the World and Throughout the Ages*. New York: Reed Press, 2004.

———. *The New Terrorism: Fanaticism and the Arms of Mass Destruction*. New York: Oxford University Press, 1999.

Leatherbarrow, W. J., ed., *Dostoevsky's The Devils: A Critical Companion*. Evanston, Ill.: Northwestern University Press, 1999.

Lewis, Bernard. "The Roots of Muslim Rage," *Policy* 17, Summer 2001-2002.

———. *What Went Wrong? Western Impact and Middle Eastern Response*. Oxford: Oxford University Press, 2002.

Lewis, C. S. *The Four Loves*. New York: Harcourt, 1988.

Lieven, Anatol. "The Cold War Is Finally Over: The True Significance of the Attacks," in James F. Hoge, Jr. and Gideon Rose, eds. *How Did This Happen?* New York: Public Affairs Reports, Council on Foreign Relations, 2001.

McCormick, Gordon H. "Terrorist Decision Making," *Annual Review of Political Science* 6, 2003.

Miller, Robin Feuer. *Imitations of Rousseau in* The Possessed, Dostoevsky Studies 5, 1984: 77-90. Found at: http://www.utoronto.ca/tsq/DS/05/077.shtml. 17 October 2008.

Muchnic, Helen. *Dostoevsky's English Reputation*. New York: Octagon Books, 1969.

Murry, J. Middleton. *Fyodor Dostoevsky: A Critical Study*. New York: Russell & Russell, 1966.

Nabokov, Vladimir. *Lectures on Russian Literature*. New York: Harcourt Brace & Company, 1981.

Naimark, Norman M. "Terrorism and the Fall of Imperial Russia," *Terrorism and Political Violence* 2, No. 2, Summer 1990.

Nechaev, Sergey. "Catechism of the Revolutionist. 1869," in Walter Laqueur, ed., *Voices of Terror: Manifestos, Writings and Manuals of Al Qaeda, Hamas, and Other Terrorists from Around the World and Throughout the Ages*. New York: Reed Press, 2004.

Orwin, Donna Tussing, *Consequences of Consciousness: Turgenev, Dostoevsky, and Tolstoy*. Stanford, Calif.: Stanford University Press, 2007.

———. "The Return to Nature: Tolstoyan Echoes in *The Idiot*," *Russian Review* 58, January 1999.

Pape, Robert A. "The Strategic Logic of Suicide Terrorism," *American Political Science Review* 97, August 2003.

Pope, Richard and Judy Turner. "Toward Understanding Stavrogin," *Slavic Review* 49, Winter 1990.

Post, Jerrold M. "Terrorist Psycho-logic: Terrorist Behavior as a Product of Psychological Forces," in Walter Reich, ed., *Origins of Terrorism: Psychologies, Ideologies, Theologies, States of Mind*. Washington, D.C.: Woodrow Wilson Center Press, 1998.

Raeff, Marc. *Origins of the Russian Intelligentsia*. New York: HBJ Book, 1966.

Rapoport, David C. "Terrorism in Three Religious Traditions, *The American Political Science Review* 78, September 1984.

Ricci, David M. *The Tragedy of Political Science*. New Haven, Conn.: Yale University Press, 1984.

Rousseau, Jean-Jacques. *Emile or On Education*, Introduction, Translation and Notes by Allan Bloom. New York: Basic Books, 1979.

———. *Julie or the New Heloise: Letters of Two Lovers Who Live in a Small Town at the Foot of the Alps*, trans. Philip Steward and Jean Vache. London: University Press of New England, 1997.

———. *The Social Contract and Discourses*. London: J. M. Dent/Everyman, 1993.

Silke, Andrew. "The Devil You Know: Continuing Problems with Research on Terrorism," *Terrorism and Political Violence* 13, Winter 2001.

Sprinzak, Ehud. "The Process of Delegitimization: Towards a Linkage Theory of Political Terrorism," *Terrorism Political Violence* 3, 1991.

———. "The Psychological Formation of Extreme Left Terrorism in a Democracy," in *Origins of Terrorism: Psychologies, Ideologies, Theologies, States of Mind*, Walter Reich, ed. Washington, D.C.: Woodrow Wilson Press, 1998.

Szamuely, Tibor. *The Russian Tradition*. London: Fontana Books, 1988.

Tocqueville, Alexis de. *Democracy in America*, trans. Harvey C. Mansfield and Delba Winthrope. Chicago: University of Chicago Press, 2002.

Tolstoy, Leo. *War and Peace*, trans. Richard Pevear and Larissa Volokhonsky. New York: Alfred A. Knopf, 2007.

Traversi, Derek. *"Dostoevsky,"* in Rene Wellek, ed, *Dostoevsky: A Collection of Critical Essays*. Englewood Cliffs, N.J.: Prentice-Hall, 1962.

Turgenev, Ivan. *Fathers and Sons*, trans. Barbara Makanowitzky. New York: Bantam Books, 1981.

Wasiolek, Edward. *Dostoevsky: The Major Fiction*. Cambridge: MIT Press, 1964.

Wellek, Rene, ed. *Dostoevsky: A Collection of Critical Essays*. Englewood Cliffs, N.J.: Prentice-Hall, 1962.

Zuckert, Catherine. "Why Political Scientists Want to Study Literature," *PS: Political Science & Politics*, June 1995.

Index

About the Author

John P. (Jack) Moran is an associate professor of political science and international affairs at Kennesaw State University just outside of Atlanta, Georgia. He is a specialist in Russian politics and international terrorism. He has also worked within this field outside of academia. While working at the U. S. Mission to the United Nations, Dr. Moran worked as liaison/action officer for UN peacekeeping operations in the former Yugoslavia (UNMOP, UNTAES, UNMIBH, UNPREDEP), Georgia (UNOMIG), and Tajikistan (UNMOT). Dr. Moran has also worked in the U. S. Embassy in Moscow, Russia, where he was responsible for translation support for the Cooperative Threat Reduction program, the Security Assistant Office, and the Office of the Defense Attache. He has also worked as a Department of the Army civilian in Tokyo, Japan, where he worked for three years as a civilian liaison officer. Most recently, he worked in the Pentagon following the 9/11 attacks as an analyst within the Joint Chiefs of Staff (J-2) and for the Undersecretary of Defense (Policy).

Among other works, Dr. Moran is the author of *From Garrison State to Nation State: Political Power and the Russian Military under Gorbachev and Yeltsin* (Praeger, 2002). He received Ph.D. and M.Phil. degrees from The George Washington University, an M.A. from the University of London, and a B.S. from Georgetown University.